AFFIXATION AND AUXILIARIES IN IGBO

In the same Series

1. Ajiboye, Oladipo. *The Syntax & Semantics of Yorùbá Nominal Expressions*
2. Anyanwu, Ogbonna Ndubuisi. *The Syntax of Igbo Causatives: A Minimalist Account*
3. Ngulube, Isaac. *The Eleme Phonology*
4. Obiamalu, Greg Orji. *Functional Categories in Igbo: A Minimalist Perspective*
5. Onumajuru, Virginia C. *Affixation and Auxiliaries in Igbo*
6. Ashipu, K.B.C. *Bette Ethnography: Theory & Practice*
7. Isaac, Baridishi Hope. *Aspects of the Grammar of Gokana*

AFFIXATION AND AUXILIARIES IN IGBO

Virginia Chinwe Onumajuru (PhD)
Senior Lecturer & Acting Head
Department of Linguistics & Communication Studies,
University of Port Harcourt, **Nigeria**

M & J Grand Orbit Communications Ltd.
Port Harcourt

The Landmarks Series Publications
Landmarks Research Foundation
Box 237 Uniport P.O.
University of Port Harcourt, **Nigeria**

e-mail: mekuri01@yahoo.com   Mobile Phone: 08033410255

Copyright © V.C. Onumajuru 2015

All rights reserved.
No part of this book may be used or reproduced in any manner, by print, photoprint, microfilm, or any other means, without the written permission from the Copyright owner except in the case of brief quotations embodied in critical articles and reviews.

ISBN: 978-978-54127-5-0

Published by

The Linguistic Association of Nigeria (LAN)

In Collaboration with

M & J Grand Orbit Communications Ltd.

Dedication

The book is dedicated to

Mama Maria and **Her Son – Jesus Christ –**

through whose inspiration it was written.

Editorial Note

The Landmarks Series is a research and publications outfit founded by the Linguistic Association of Nigeria (LAN), and solely funded by the Landmarks Research Foundation to publish recently completed and outstanding doctoral theses on any aspect of Nigerian linguistics, languages, literature, communication and cultures. The purpose is to encourage the circulation of ideas generated by theses written by members of the Linguistic Association of Nigeria (LAN). It is hoped that the opportunity to publish in the Landmark Series might be extended to non-members of LAN in due course.

The fifth edition in the series is the revised version of Dr. (Mrs.) Virginia Chinwe Onumajuru's doctoral thesis which was submitted to the Department of Linguistics and Communication Studies, University of Port Harcourt, Nigeria. The work focuses on affixation and auxiliaries in the Ọnịcha variety of Igbo. It identifies prefixes, suffixes, interfixes, circumfixes, super/suprafixes, extensional suffixes among the affixes in the variety of Igbo that she studied. The work is presented in two sections: Section 1 discusses affixation, while Section 2 is focused on auxiliary verbs.

Section 1 is further divided into five chapters, while Section 2 is a single chapter. Chapter 1 is a general introduction that provides some background information regarding Ọnịcha Igbo and the speakers of the lect. Chapter 2 an overview of affixation as an important word formation process in world languages. Chapter 3 is the morpho-syntactic analysis of inflectional affixes. Chapter 4 discusses the morpho-syntactic characteristics of derivational affixes, while Chapter 5 is concerned with the morpho-syntactic as well as the semantic charateristics of verbal extensions in Igbo.

Section 2 is a sole chapter which discusses in a systematic manner the different types of auxiliary verbs, their uses and the effect of their co-occurrence with perfective verb forms.

All those interested in affixation and related phenomena in Igboid studies and beyond will find this book an excellent companion. The book is written in lucid prose that both straightforward and elegant. Granted it grew out of a PhD thesis, it is totally devoid of technical jargons. It is an easy-to-follow text. I strongly recommend it to researchers in search of a simple text on morphology.

Ozo-mekuri Ndimele, PhD
Professor of Comparative Grammar & Communications
Founding Editor & Fmr. National President,
Linguistic Association of Nigeria
August 2015

Preface

This book derives largely from my PhD thesis which I defended at the Department of Linguistics and Communication Studies, University of Port Harcourt, in October 2007. The book is in two sections; the first section discusses affixation in Ọnịcha Igbo. It comprises five chapters. Chapter 1 deals with some preliminary remarks; Chapter 2 makes a general review of affixation as a word formation process; Chapter 3 is the morpho-syntactic analysis of inflectional affixes; Chapter 4 examines a morpho-syntactic analysis of derivational affixes and chapter 5 is a discussion of the morpho-syntactic analysis of extensional suffixes. The second section comprises a single chapter article entitled Auxiliaries in Igbo whose earlier version was published in the *Language and Economic Reforms in Nigeria*.

The motivation for the book is the realization that little or no serious research work has been done on the Ọnịcha Igbo variety compared to some other Igbo varieties, and this is a serious lack considering the status of Onitsha south of the Niger. The Ọnịcha dialect was the version used by the missionaries in the work of evangelization in Igboland in the late nineteenth century before the advent of the present Standard Igbo variety. With the emergence of the Standard Igbo, it appears that Ọnịcha Igbo was relegated to the background.

Many people contributed towards ensuring a successful completion of this book, and I wish to express my sincere gratitude to such personalities. Prominent among them are my supervisors, Professor Ozo-mekuri Ndimele and Professor (Mrs) P.E. Ejele who meticulously and diligently supervised the work. I pray for God's choicest blessings on them.

My unalloyed thanks go to all my other lectuerers who also contributed in my formation as a linguist. They include the Late Professor Kay Willianson, Professor E.N. Emenanjo, Professor (Mrs) Shirley Yul-Ifode and Dr. C. E. W. Jenewari. I sincerely appreciate my classmate and friend Dr. (Mrs) Esther Nwakaego Oweleke who is also a close research associate. I thank God for the cause that brought us together. I cannot adequately express my gratitude to my sister and friend Dr. (Mrs) C.I. Omego, former Acting Head of the Department of Linguistics and Communication Studies and a research collaborator and colleague. To the many lecturers of the Department of Linguistics and Communication Studies, I say thank you for the team work we have enjoyed.

My sincere appreciation goes to all my family friends and well wishers who showed keen interest in the progress of this book. I must not fail to mention Rev. Fr. Professor C.I. Ejizu and Rev. Fr. Professor B.E. Nwigwe for their support and encouragement throughout the course of this work. You are truly *the good sherpherds*. I thank also the following for their sincere support and encouragement: Sir & Lady (Dr.) J J Mezie-Okoye, Mr & Mrs C.C. Mezie-Okoye, Professor Tony Arinze, Professor & Mrs C.E. Nnolim, Professor & Mrs C. T. Maduka, Professor & Dr. (Mrs) C.O. Umeozor, Mr &

Dr. (Mrs) Odii Onyido, Chief Mrs B.I. Nzimiro (*B the Best*), Rev. Fr Dr. Goody Okeke and Rev. Fr. C.C. Adinuba.

I must not forget to mention Professor E.O. Ayalogu, former Deputy Vice-Chancellor (Administration), University of Port Harcourt, for the efforts he made to organize informants for me.

I am greatly indebted to my husband, Dr. E.M. Onumajuru (*the Saint*) for his all-round support and encouragement. May the Almighty God bless and keep you. And for my children and dependants, my brothers and sisters, I pray for God's abundant blessings on all of you.

Finally, I pray for the eternal repose of my beloved parents, Mr. Aloysius and Mrs Rebecca Oliobi Ichoku, and also for my many brothers and sisters who have paid the supreme debt. May you rest in the bosom of the Lord. Amen.

Table of Contents

Dedication	v
Editorial Note	vi
Preface	vii
List of Abbreviations and Conventions	xiii

Chapter 1

The Igbo language and its speakers	1
1.1 The Igbo language	1
1.2 The Igbo people – Ndigbo	2
1.2.1 The origin of Ndigbo	2
1.3 The origin and geographical location of the Ọnịcha speakers	3
1.3.1 The origin of the Ọnịcha	3
1.3.2 Geographical location of the Ọnịcha people	4
1.3.3 The linguistic situation of Ọnịcha	5
1.4 Brief statement on the sound system	5
1.4.1 The vowel system	5
1.4.2 The vowel harmony	7
1.5 The Consonant system	8
1.6 The syllable structure	8
1.7 The Igbo tonal system	9

Chapter 2

Affixation as a word formation process	11
2. Introduction	11
2.1 Definition of related terms	13
2.1.1 Morphology	13
2.1.2 Morphme	13
2.1.3 Affix	13
2.1.4 Affixation	14
2.1.5 Root	14
2.1.6 Stem	15
2.1.7 Base	15
2.2 Classification of affixes	15
2.2.1 Positional classification of affixes	15
2.2.2. Functional classification of affixes	15
2.3 Distinction between inflectional and derivational affixes	16
2.3.1 Configurational properties	18
2.3.2 Agreement properties	19
2.3.3 Inherent properties	19
2.3.4 Phrasal properties	19
2.4 The nature of words	20
2.5 Illustration of affixation process using different languages	20
2.5.1 Number	20

2.5.2 Negation	21
2.5.3 Nominal derivation	22
2.5.4 Verbal derivatives	22
2.5.4.1 Infix	22
2.5.4.2 Interfix	22
2.5.4.3 Circumfix	22
2.5.4.4 Super/Suprafix	24
2.6. Processes of affixation in Igbo	25
2.6.1 Classification of Igbo verbs	27
2.6.1.1 Active verbs	27
2.6.1.2 Stative verb	27
2.7 Affixes as important elements of derivation in Igbo	29
2.7.1 Deverbatives	29
2.7.2 Verbal deverbatives	30
2.7.3 Derivational morphology	30
2.7.4 Interfixation as a derivational process in Igbo	31
2.7.5 Suffixation as part of derivational process in Ọnịcha	32
2.7.6 Inflectional affixes	34
2.7.7 Extensional suffixes	35

Chapter 3 — 37
Morpho-syntactic analysis of inflectional affixe — 37

3. Introduction	37
3.1 Inflectional affixes in indicative constructions	38
3.1.1 Inflectional affixes in the indicative affirmative constructions	38
3.1.1.1 =LV Benefactive	39
3.1.2 Inflectional affixes in the indicative negative constructions	41
3.2 Inflectional affixes in imperative constructions	42
3.2.1 The imperative affirmative	42
3.2.2 The imperative negative	44
3.3 Inflectional affixes in imperfective constructions	45
3.3.1 The present continuous form	45
3.3.1.1 The present progressive form	45
3.3.1.2 The present Imminent form	47
3.3.2 The expression of the future form	49
3.4 Inflectional affixes in Perfective constructions	51
3.4.1 The future Perfective	52
3.4.2. The present perfective	53
3.4.3 The past perfective	54
3.4.4 The unfulfilled perfective	55
3.5 Recapitulatory table of inflectional verbal affixes in Ọnịcha Igbo	58

Chapter 4
Morpho-syntactic analysis of derivational affixes 61
4. Introduction 61
4.1 Prefixation 62
4.1.1 The infinitive 62
4.1.2 The participle 66
4.1.3 Prefixation and reduplication 68
4.1.4 Prefixation and suffixation 69
4.2 Interfixation 70
4.2.1 The noun-base form of interfixation 71
4.3 Circumfixation 73
4.4.1 Bound Cognate Noun (BCN) 74
4.4.2 Gerund 77
4.4.3 Noun Agents 78
4.4.4 Noun instruments 79
4.4.5 Noun of Results 81
4.4.6 Miscellaneous deverbatives 83
4.5 Tone as a derivative morpheme in Ọnịcha Igbo 87
4.5.1 Tone in sentences 89
4.5.2 Functions of tones in derivation 91
4.6 Summary of derivational affixes in the Ọnịcha dialect of Igbo 93

Chapter 5 95
Morpho-syntactic analysis of extensional suffixes 95
5. Introduction 95
5.1 Features of extensional suffix in Ọnịcha Igbo 96
5.2 Extensional suffix and verb root 96
5.3 Extensional suffix and enclitics 98
5.4 An analysis of the extensional suffixes in Ọnịcha Igbo 99
5.4.1 Imperativeness 99
5.4.2 Temporality 101
5.4.2.1 Anteriority extenders 101
5.4.2.2 Frequentative extenders 102
5.4.2.3 Durative extenders 102
5.4.3 Direction extenders 103
5.4.3.1 Motive extenders 103
5.4.3.2 Dative extenders 105
5.4.3.3 Locative extenders 106
5.4.3.4 Benefactive extenders 107
5.4.4 Contact function 108
5.4.4.1 Fellowship extenders 108
5.4.4.2 Fixative extenders 109
5.4.4.3 Touch extenders 110

5.4.5 Evaluation	111
5.4.5.1 Comparative extenders	112
5.4.5.2 Partial extenders	113
5.4.5.3 Relief extenders	113
5.4.6 Reflexives	114
5.4.6.1 Revisory extender	114
5.4.6.2 Retaliative extender	115
5.4.7 Termination	116
5.4.7.1 Completive extenders	116
5.4.7.2 Conclusive extenders	117
5.4.8 Miscellaneous	118
5.4.8.1 Causative extenders	118
5.4.8.2 Primal extender	120
5.4.8.3 Dispositinal extenders	121
5.5 Co-occurrence possibilities of extensional suffixes	123
5.5.1 Order of extensional suffixes	126
5.5.2 Order of extensional and inflectional suffixes	129
Chapter 6	**133**
Auxiliaries in Igbo	**133**
6. Introduction	133
6.1 Primary Auxiliary	135
6.2 Modal Auxiliary	136
6.2.1 Modal auxiliary and perfective verb forms	138
6.3 Conclusion	142
References	**145**
Subject Index	**151**

Chapter 1

The Igbo Language and its Speakers

1.1 The Igbo Language

The Igbo language according to the classifications of Bennett and Sterk (1977) in Bendor-Samuel (1989:261) belongs to the Igboid group of languages of the Benue-Congo which is one of the sub-families of the Niger-Congo family. Igbo is one of the three main Nigerian languages and it is dialectically highly diversified.

Speaking on the multiplicity of dialects in Igbo, Nwadike (1981:22) states that the language is fraught with multi-dialects which can be grouped in clusters thus: Ika, Ukwuani, and Enuani clusters (in Delta state), Onitsha, Orlu, Owerri, Nsukka, Umuahia, Abakaliki, Oguta clusters (in Anambra, Imo, Enugu, Ebonyi, and Abia states) and Ikwere-Echie cluster (in Rivers state). Nwadike's list is not exhaustive but it shows how diversified the Igbo dialects are. It has to be emphasized, however, that all the dialects in a given cluster are not similar in all respects. They share degrees of 'intercomprehensibility' among themselves but have some grammatical, lexical, and phonological differences.

Ejiofor (1982:11), affirming Nwadike's observation on the dialects of Igbo, zones Igbo along cultural lines, as follows:

- Cultural zones among the Igbo
- The main divisions of the Igbo-speaking peoples
- The composition of the Southern or Owerri Igbo
- The composition of the Western Igbo – Ika
- The composition of the Eastern or Cross-River Igbo.

Units	Cultural Area	General Name
I	Northern or Onitsha Igbo	Onitsha
II	Southern or Owerri Igbo	Owerri
III	Western Igbo	Ika
IV	Eastern or Cross-River Igbo	Aro and Abriba
V	North-Eastern Igbo	Izza

Table 1–I Cultural zones among the Igbo as presented by Ejiofor

Below follows a representation of the main divisions of the Igbo-speaking peoples:

Main Division	Administrative Area	Linguistic Designation
Western/Nri Awka	Onitsha, Awka	Onitsha Igbo
Eastern or Enugu	Nsukka, Udi, Awgu, Okigwe	Nsukka, Wawa Igbo
Onitsha town	Onitsha	Onitsha Igbo

Table 1–II Composition of the Northern or Ọnịcha Igbo

Isu-Ama	Okigwe, Orlu, Owerri	Owerri Igbo
Oratta-Ikwerre	Owerri, Ahoada	Owerri and Ikwerre Igbo
Ohuhu Ngwa	Aba, Bende	Ngwa Igbo
Isu-Item	Bende, Okigwe	Abriba Igbo

Table 1–III Composition of the Southern or Owerri Igbo

Northern Ika	Ogwashi uku, Agbor	Ika Igbo
Southern Ika or Kwale	Kwale	Ika Igbo
Riverain	Ogwashi uku, W. Onitsha, S. Owerri, Ahoada	Olu Igbo

Table 1–IV Composition of the Western or Ika Igbo

Ada (Elda)	Afikpo	Abriba Igbo
Abam – Ohafia	Bende, Okigwe	Abriba Igbo
Aro	Aro	Abriba Igbo

Table 1–V Composition of the Eastern or Cross River Igbo

Okeke (1984:25), still commenting on the various varieties of the Igbo language, asserts that the most prominent of the dialects are the Onitsha and the Owere dialect (-al) groupings.

Confirming the assertion by Okeke, Echeruo (1998: XV) adds:

> In general, there are two major dialect zones in Igbo: Owere and Onitsha, although quite significant variations occur within each zone. Indeed, the zones are defined by a general combination of syntactical, lexical, and phonological features rather than exclusively by any one of those elements.

1.2 The Igbo People – Ndigbo
1.2.1 The Origin of Ndigbo

The origin of Ndigbo remains controversial as no authoritative research can be cited yet. Afigbo (1986:1) puts forward some hypotheses on the origin of Ndigbo which can be summarized as follows:

i. Ndigbo broke off from their Kwa brothers in the region of the Niger-Benue confluence and from there moved down to their present habitat.

ii. Ndigbo were created where they are now found – autochthonous existence.

iii. Ndigbo were one of the tribes of Israel or of Egypt and for some reason, they left the East, wandered across the Sudan, and settled where they are now found.

iv. Ndigbo should be traced to the Nri of Awka. This version is the most detailed of the claims of origin of Ndigbo. Ndigbo believe Nri in Awka and Amaigbo in Orlu to be their spiritual and ideological metropolis from where different sects moved to their present locations. While the Western and Northern Ndigbo believe that the souls of their dead walk the streets of Nri on their way to the realm populated by the revered ancestors, the other Igbo groups such as the Ohuhu, Ngwa, Mbaise, or even the Cross-River Igbo believe that Amaigbo in Orlu represents what Nri stands for among Northern and Western Ndigbo.

1.3 Origin and Geographical Location of the Ọnịcha Dialect Speakers
1.3.1 The Origin of the Ọnịcha People
The story of the origin of the Ọnịcha people has been variously presented by scholars. Two major concepts are adopted by the Ọnịcha people in referring to the origin of their community. The concepts are as follows:

i. The notion of *Ebo Itenani* – nine clans
ii. *Umu-Eze-Chima* Children of King Chima

The above are the two different and incompatible perspectives from which the Ọnịcha people view their origin. Oral traditions within the descent group framework maintain that Ọnịcha was fundamentally heterogeneous in its origins, including elements of riverain Ibo, Igala speakers, Awka-Orlu upland Ibo, Western Ibo, and possibly others (Henderson 1972:76). The degree of the diversity or homogeneity of the origin of the Ọnịcha people is determined by the point of view the narrator wants to emphasize. For instance, if the intention of the narrator is to highlight the diversity of the origin of the Ọnịcha people, he adopts the *Ebo Itenani* nine clans legend which states that Ọnịcha people are descendants of different clans with nine distinct kings. If, on the other hand, the narrator intends to stress the homogeneous whole of the Ọnịcha people, he uses the notion of *Umu-Eze-Chima* or children of King Chima which states that Ọnịcha people migrated from Bini (Ado and Idu) under the leadership of a glorious founder-king, Chima. The synthesis of these elements into a coherent tradition can only be understood by reference to the unifying effects of kingship.

1.3.2 Geographical Location of the Ọnịcha People

Fig 1-I Map of Southern Nigeria showing Ọnịcha and its environs above the Niger Delta

Onitsha is bounded on the north by Nkwelle-Ezunaka and the less well-known town, Onono. It is bounded on the south by Iyiowa Odekpe, on the east by Ikenga Ogidi, and on the west by the Niger River.

Onitsha is one of the major cities of Anambra state in the southeast zone of Nigeria. Perched on the east bank of the Niger river and the gateway to Anambra state from Asaba, capital city of Delta state, Onitsha is situated at 6°N and 6.42 °E, occupies a landmass of 20 square kilometers, and has a population of 362, 700 (1995 estimate). For administrative purposes, Onitsha is divided into two local government areas known as Onitsha North and Onitsha South. The town, Onitsha, with nine villages, is made up of thirty council wards. It houses the biggest imposing market in West Africa known as the *Onitsha Main Market*. It has a very busy road transportation network to all parts of Nigeria. It is a good example of a conurbation as it has expanded on all its frontiers to assimilate other lesser known towns with the result that towns like Nkpor, Ogidi, Oba, Obosi, etc are sometimes referred to as Onitsha.

1.3.3 Linguistic situation of Ọnịcha

Ọnịcha dialect has two varieties: the one spoken by the Onitsha indigenes, which Williamson(1972:xii) refers to as a highly specialized form, and which Emenanjo (1976) calls the original Ọnịcha dialect, spoken by the 'sons of the soil'(who live at Enu-Onitsha, or Onitsha hinterland), and the widely understood and used dialect spoken by the traders and non-indigenes of Onitsha, which Williamson refers to as the generalized form, and which Emenanjo refers to as Ọnịcha Igbo, spoken by mixed populations in the major trading areas of Onitsha. This book is based on the generalized version of the Ọnịcha dialect.

NB: the major difference between the speech forms of the two varieties of the Ọnịcha Igbo is that the *highly specialized form otherwise called the original Ọnịcha dialect* replaces the phoneme 'f' with the phoneme 'v' such that words like 'afa, afọ etc.' are pronounced 'ava, avọ etc.' respectively by the Onicha indigenes.

1.4 Brief Statement on Sound System

Here, we review the Ọnịcha dialect sound system with respect to its vowels and consonants. It would be erroneous to presume that the Central Igbo dialect speech sounds currently in use must apply integrally to all Igbo dialects including Ọnịcha. In Igbo, it is an established fact that dialects differ from one another in many respects, including their lexicon and phonological features. For instance, whereas some dialects are associated with the phonological characteristics of aspiration and nasalization, others are not.

However, our aim is not to undertake an elaborate study of the Ọnịcha phonological system, but to identify the basic speech sounds which can be used to describe the dialect adequately.

1.4.1 The Vowel Sounds

In his *Aspects of the Phonology and Morphology of Ọnịcha (A Dialect of Igbo)*, Emenanjo (1976:21) states that there are ten phonetic vowels in the Ọnịcha dialect which *fall into two mutually exclusive sets in accordance with their tendency to co-occur*. They are as follow:

Set A [ɪ, ɛ, ɔ, a⁺, ʊ]
Set B [i, e, o, a⁻, u]

Following his phonological analysis to determine the status of the above ten phonetic vowels, Emenanjo (1976:25) concludes that Ọnịcha dialect has eight phonemic vowels which he outlines thus:

/ ị, i, e, a, o, ọ, u, ụ/

He further states that these eight vowels fall superficially into two vowel harmony patterns set out as follows:

Group 1	Group 2
i, o, u	i̧, o̧, u̧
e	a

Before reaching the above conclusion, Emenanjo (1976:22-23) states that [ɛ] and [e], though without any attested minimal pairs, are, by complementary distribution, allophones of the same phoneme, to be symbolized as /e/. It is, however, pertinent to indicate that his choice of [e] as the archiphoneme is arbitrary because, judging from his analyses [ɛ] has wider distribution than [e] and should have been chosen as the major phoneme. He also states that [a⁺] and [aˉ], for which there are no minimal pairs, are, by complementary distribution, allophones of the same phoneme, to be symbolized as /a/. The other six phonemic vowels, namely [i, ɪ, u, u̧, o, ɔ], are, according to Emenanjo (1976:22), confirmed to have phonemic status through minimal pair combinations. The overall resultant effect is the above eight vowel vocalic system for the Ọnịcha dialect.

Creissels (1989:84) differs slightly from Emenanjo on the composition of the Ọnịcha vocalic system. According to Creissels (1989:84), the Ọnịcha dialect has nine phonetic vowels (i, ɪ, e, ɛ, a, ɔ, o, ʊ, u), eight of which are phonemic, namely /i, ɪ, ɛ, a, u, ʊ, o, ɔ/. Like Emenanjo (1976), Creissels (1989) maintains that [e] and [ẹ] are allophones of the same phoneme. But, whereas Creissels symbolizes these allophones as the phoneme /ɛ/, based on its greater distribution, Emenanjo (1976: 22-23) symbolizes them as /e/, despite its lesser distribution. How do we resolve these contradictions in order to forge ahead?

Creissels (1989:84) presents his summary of the Ọnịcha phonemic vowels as /i, ɪ, ɛ, a, u, u̧, o, ɔ/ with the derivation rule /ɛ/ → e when followed by either i, u, or o within the same word. However, from the separate studies of Creissels (1989) and Emenanjo (1976), we make the following observations with respect to the phonological status of [ɛ] and [e] in Ọnịcha dialect:

i. [ɛ] can co-occur with all the non-expanded vowels and with itself.
ii. [ɛ] can co-occur as the unique vowel of monosyllabic lexemes, (example jɛ́ *go*) and in two or more syllabic lexemes in which the non-expanded vowels are in harmony.
iii. [ɛ] co-occurs profusely with nominals, verbals, and nomino-verbals.
iv. [e] can co-occur with all the expanded vowels (example ego *money*) but not with itself in the same word (example ege*).
v. [e] cannot occur as the unique vowel in monosyllabic verbal lexemes (example jé*).
vi. [e] can co-occur with nominals with the other expanded vowels, but not with itself.
vii. [e] can co-occur with the nominal-verbal (or participle) as participial prefix but cannot co-occur with itself.

From the above analyses concerning the distribution of [ɛ] and [e], a close observation reveals that [ɛ] has wider distribution than [e] in the Ọnịcha dialect and should therefore be regarded ipso facto as the phonemic vowel, as recommended by Creissels (1989). In this work, we shall adopt, for the Ọnịcha dialect, Creissels' eight phoneme vocalic system with its rule for the realization of the vowel [e] as stated above. [ɛ] and [e] are therefore allophones of the same vowel represented as /ɛ/.

The summary of the co-occurrence of [e] and [ɛ] in the Ọnịcha Igbo vocalic system can be represented thus the simple rule goes as follows:

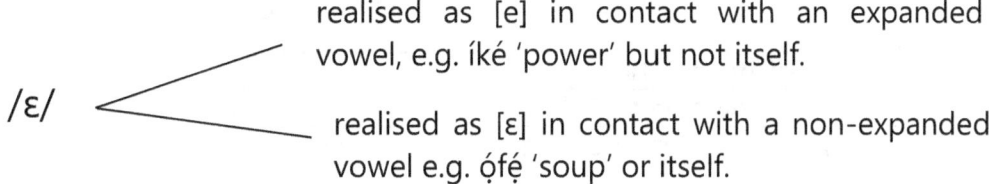

Below is a representation of the vocalic system of the Ọnịcha variety of Igbo.

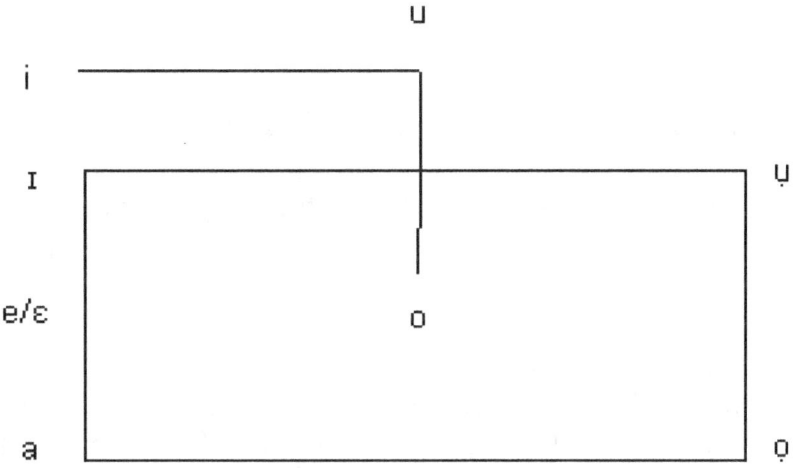

Fig 1-II Onumajuru's representation of the Ọnịcha vocalic system (cf. Onumajuru 2005:695)

1.4.2 Vowel Harmony

The vowel harmony is a system whereby the vowels are divided into two sets, *wide* and *narrow*, in such a way that vowels from the same sets normally go together in the same simple word(Williamson1984:70). The vowels in Ọnịcha Igbo (indeed in Igbo language) divide fairly into two harmony groups (wide & narrow sets) such that only vowels of one group may co-occur. The vowels of each group are produced by the corresponding movement and position of the root of the tongue hence the *Advanced Root Tongue* phenomenon. The vowels in the wide set otherwise called the expanded vowels are produced with an expanded pharynx [+ATR], while the vowels in the narrow set are produced with non-expanded pharynx [-ATR]. The vowel harmony system of the Ọnịcha dialect corresponds to that of the Standard Igbo dialect except that the Ọnịcha system has, in addition, a retracted vowel [ẹ] which makes it distinct from the Standard Igbo dialect. Elsewhere in this work, we have discussed the co-occurrence of vowels in the dialect and we conclude here by saying that there is harmony in the co-occurrence of vowels in the Ọnịcha variety of Igbo.

1.4.3 The Consonant System
There are twenty-six consonants in the Ọnịcha dialect of Igbo. They are almost the same as the consonants in the Central Igbo dialect except for the predominant presence in the Central Igbo dialect of the glottal sound /h/. The labio-dental fricative sound /f/ in Ọnịcha replaces the glottal sound in Central Igbo. If the glottal sound /h/ is removed from the Central Igbo dialect, what we have for both Ọnịcha and Central Igbo consonant systems are very identical. Below is the Williamson chart of the Ọnịcha Igbo dialect.

Mode of Articulation	Place of Articulation				
	Labial	Alveolar	Palatal	Velar	Labialized Velar
Plosive	p b	t d	ch j	k g	kw gw
Implosive	kp gb				
Nasal	m	n	ny	ñ	nw
Fricative	f	s	(z) (sh)	gh	
Tap/Roll		r			
Lateral		l			
Approximant			y		w

Table 1–XI The Williamson chart of the Ọnịcha Igbo dialect (cf. 1972:lxiv) as adapted.

The above chart shows that the phoneme [h], which is very prominent in the Central Igbo dialect, is not attested to in the Ọnịcha dialect, except in exclamations, as recorded by Williamson (1972).

The phoneme [v] (voiced labio-dental fricative), which is attested in both the Central Igbo dialect and in the highly specialized form of Ọnịcha dialect, is not attested in the generalized form of Ọnịcha dialect. It is the phoneme [f] (voiceless labio-dental fricative) that does the job in the Ọnịcha variety. We observe, from the chart, that Williamson (1972) omitted the phoneme [z] (voiced alveolar fricative) which is attested in the dialect in words like: úzọ̀ *way/door*; àzú *back/behind*; ázụ̀ *fish*, etc. we have therefore enclosed [z] within parentheses in Williamson's Ọnịcha chart.

As we observe from the Ọnịcha sound system (vowel and consonant) above, there is neither aspiration nor nasalization in either of them.

1.5 The Syllable Structure
A syllable is according to Crystal (1997:373) defined as a *unit of pronunciation typically larger than a single sound and smaller than a word*. It can be described as the peak of sonority. The syllabic structure in Ọnịcha Igbo variety corresponds to the syllabic typology of the Igbo language which is represented as CV, CVCV. For instance the following extensional suffixes can be represented syllabically as:

- =ba/=be inceptive (CV)
- =gide/=dide persistent (CVCV)
- =lili/=lịlị persistent (CVCV)
- =kọ associative (CV)

1.6 The Igbo Tonal System

A tone is a meaning-making element in some languages. It is a systematic variation of the voice pitch used by languages to distinguish both lexical and grammatical meanings. Igbo is a tonal language, and all its dialects, including Ọnịcha, are tonal. In Ọnịcha, the tone carried by a word is an essential feature of its meaning.

Ọnịcha, like other Igbo dialects, has three lexical tones which are represented thus:

- High [']
- Low [`]
- Downstep [¯] in isolation; ['] in construction

The high and low tones can occur in every environment initial, middle, and final positions. The downstep can neither occur at the initial position nor can it follow a low tone. It occurs only as a final tone in a disyllabic word as in the following words:

- élō   *mushroom*
- álū   *abomination*
- égō   *money*

Two basic tones, the high and low tones, are, however, freely distributed in Ọnịcha. In combination, the three lexical tones are subsumed under high and low tones because the downstep is itself raised to a high tone though the *height* of the *elevation* does not match that of the preceding high tone.

Chapter 2

Affixation as a Word Formation Process

2. Introduction

The chapter provides background information on affixation as a word-formation process. Particular attention will be paid to affixation as it applies to the Igbo language.

Morphological constructions are products of affixation and compounding. They are very important elements in human language.

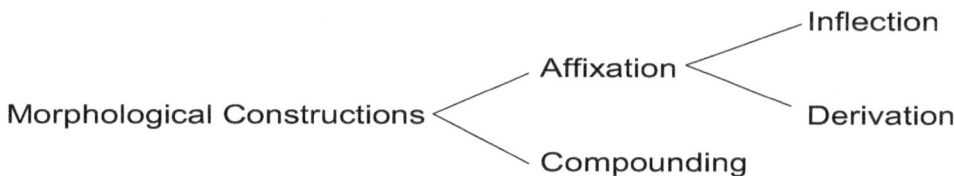

Affixation is one of the two major traditional processes of word formation, the other being compounding. Affixation entails the addition of an affix to a stem to yield a complex stem, while compounding involves adding two or more stems together to form a single word.

The formation of a word may involve the application of more than one morphological process. For instance, in the formation of a word like *self-consciousness* in the English language, the first morphological process involved is that of compounding which joins the simple stems *self* and *conscious* to form a compound stem *self-conscious*. To this is added the suffix *–ness* to yield the derivation *self-consciousness* which is a product of compounding and affixation.

In the literature, the term *affixation* evokes inflection and derivation. It is concerned with the concatenation of affixes. Inflection is defined in classical grammatical theory as:

> … a change made in the form of a word to express its relation to other words in the sentence. And in the grammars of particular language the section on inflection will describe the declensions of nouns, adjectives, pronouns and the conjugations of verbs according to selected models of formation or paradigms (Lyons 1968:195)

There are two divisions of word formation in both compounding and derivation. Compounding breaks up into two parts namely, primary (or root compounding) and synthetic (or verbal compounding), while derivation is sometimes subdivided into class-maintaining and class-changing derivations.

Class-maintaining derivation is the derivation of new lexemes which are of the same form class (part of speech) as the base from which they are formed.

Examples:

Stem	Prefix	Derivative
Take	re-	Retake
Please	dis-	Displease
Admission	re-	Readmission
Admissible	in-	Inadmissible

Table 1-VI Class-maintaining derivatives

The first two examples are verbs both before and after the derivation while the last two are noun and adjective respectively. In other words, no change has taken place in them from the point of view of form class.

The class-changing derivation, on the other hand, produces lexemes which belong to different word classes from their bases, for example:

Stem	Suffix	Derivative
Teach	-er	Teacher
Nation	-al	National

Table 1-VII Class-changing derivatives

We observe from the examples that the base and the derivatives belong to different word classes, thereby justifying the term *class-changing derivation*.

Derivation lists various processes whereby new words are formed from existing words or roots. For example, the adjective *seasonal* is derived from the noun *season* and the noun *instruction* is derived from the verb *instruct*. The adjective *acceptable*, is derived from the verb *accept*.

In Igbo studies, the terms *affix* and *affixation* have received the attention of analysts. Just as in other agglutinating languages, word formation/ creation in Igbo is achieved through affixation and compounding. In compounding, as already mentioned above, two independent Igbo words can be combined to form a single word. For instance, nominals can combine to form nouns and verbals can also combine to form verbs, as in the following examples:

Nominals

Noun 1	Noun 2	Compound Noun
ọnyẹ *person*	ńkuzi *teaching*	ọnyẹ ńkuzi *teacher*
nwátà *child*	ákwụ́kwọ́ *book*	nwátà ákwụ́kwọ́ *student*

Table 1-VIII Nominals formed by compounding

Verbals		
Verb 1	Verb 2	Compound Verb
bú carry	pụ̀ go out	búpụ̀ carry out
gbú kill	dà fall down	gbúdà cut down

Table 1-IX Verbals formed by compounding

In derivation, the verb root combines with affixes to yield a form or a derivative, as in the following examples:

Verb Root	Infinitive	Noun	Gerundive
kwú speak	íkwū to speak	ókwú speech	òkwúkwú act of speaking

Table 1-X Derivatives formed through affixation

2.1 Definitions of related terms
2.1.1 Morphology
Lyons (1968:195) states that morphology was introduced into linguistics in the 19th century to cover both inflection and derivation. Before this time, the term had first been applied in biology to the study of the forms of living organisms. It was later applied to linguistics to refer to the study of the shapes of words, the systematic changes in shapes related to changes in meaning. It is used for the collection of units which are used in changing the forms of words. By extension, morphology is used for the sequence of rules which are postulated by linguists to account for the changes in the shapes of words. Newmeyer (1990:146) defines morphology as the study of the structure of words and of the ways in which their structure reflects their relation to other words – both within some larger construction such as a sentence and across the total vocabulary of the language. Crystal (1997:249) defines morphology as the branch of grammar which studies the structure or forms of words, primarily through the use of the morpheme construct.

From the above definitions, we observe that Newmeyer and Crystal have identical views of the application of the term *morphology* in linguistics.

2.1.2 Morpheme
Bloomfield (1933:161) defines *morpheme* as the elemental unit of morphological analysis. Katamba (1993:20) also defines *morpheme* as a term which refers to the smallest, indivisible unit of semantic content or grammatical function which words are made up of. He identifies two types of morphemes – free morphemes and bound morphemes. The free morphemes are the lexical morphemes which carry semantic content of utterances. Katamba refers to bound morphemes as affixes, grammatical morphemes, or function words which signal grammatical information or logical relations in a sentence.

2.1.3 Affix
Trask (1993:1), Katamba (1993:44), Rodman and Fromkin (1998:71) define affix as a bound morpheme which can only occur attached to a word or stem as distinct from

free morphemes. Ndimele (2001:16) also defines affix as a bound morpheme which is not capable of independent existence. It must be attached to another linguistic unit. Emenanjo (1978:215) and Ejele (1996:83) apply the term to smallest meaningful grammatical elements that are added to the root.

From the above definitions of affixes, we can conclude that affixes are added to roots, either to single morphemes occurring as free morphemes or to various combinations of morphemes. Affixes can occur at the beginning, at the middle, or at the end of a word.

2.1.4 Affixation

Crystal (1997:12) defines affixation as a morphological process whereby grammatical or lexical information is added to a stem. He describes affixal morphology as an approach which claims that the only permissible morphological operation is the combining of affixes and stems.

Matthews (1974:124) gives a slightly different definition of affixation. He states that affixation is a process whereby the derivand (the form which results when a process or operation is applied) will consist of the operand (the form that is applied to) plus a new formative which has been added or affixed to it. Schematically, Matthews represents affixation thus:

$$O \rightarrow O + ed$$

where **O** stands for any possible operands and the single constant **–ed** (or any of its variants) is added to all. By Matthews' definition, the terms derivand, operand, and new formative represent the terms derivative, root (or base) and affix respectively. Affixation therefore is the process of attaching affixes to a base in order to derive or form a new word.

2.1.5 Root

Bauer (1989:20) defines a root as a form which is not further analyzable either in terms of derivational or inflectional morphology. It is that part of a word-form that remains when all inflectional and derivational affixes have been removed. A root, according to Anagbogu (2001:103) is an uninflected morpheme to which an affix can be attached. Katamba (1993:4) also defines a root as the irreducible core of a word with absolutely nothing attached to it. It is the part that is always present with some modifications of a lexeme.

Eka (2004:64) gives ways of looking at the word root:

- A root can be used to mean a morpheme of word status
- It can also be used to explain the origin of a word from another language. He says that a root can serve as a base but not every base can be a root.

The above definitions of a root from different linguists show that a root is the central or core part of the word which remains after every other linguistic unit has been removed.

2.1.6 Stem
A stem is according to Bauer (1989:20), that part of the word-form which remains when all inflectional affixes have been removed. A stem may be complex in that it may contain more than one root. It may contain derivational but not inflectional affixes.

2.1.7 Base
Bauer (1989:21) defines a base as any form to which affixes of any kind can be added. In other words, any root or any stem can be termed a base.

2.2 Classification of Affixes
Two main criteria have been identified in the literature for the classification of affixes. They are:

a. the position an affix occupies vis-à-vis the root of the word
b. the function an affix performs when added to the root/base of a word

2.2.1 Positional Classification of Affixes
With respect to the positional classification of affixes, Ndimele (1999:22ff) lists the following as examples of affixes in the human language:

a. *Prefix:* when the affix occurs before the root or base of a word
b. *Suffix:* when the affix occurs after the root or base of a word
c. *Infix:* when the affix is incorporated inside the root of a word
d. *Interfix:* when the affix occurs between two identical or non-identical roots
e. *Circumfix:* when the affix surrounds the root of the word i.e. the first half of the affix occurs before the root and the second half occurs after the root.
f. *Supra-/Superfix:* when the affix is marked over the syllables that form part of a root. Superfix comes in the form of tones or stress marks placed over words.

2.2.2 Functional Classification of Affixes
From the point of view of functional classification of affixes, Katamba (1993:45), Spencer (1997:21), and Ndimele (1999:36) distinguish between derivational and inflectional affixes while Nwachukwu (1983:61) discusses affixes under inflectional and non-inflectional types. Basing his findings on the Igbo language, Nwachukwu argues that Igbo affixes do not fall into a neat classification of inflectional and derivational, as in Indo-European linguistics. For clarity, affixes are classified functionally in the literature into three namely:

-inflectional
-derivational
-extensional

2.3 Distinction between Inflectional & Derivational Affixes

Linguists, including Jespersen (1924), Bybee (1985), Spencer (1991), and Katamba (1993), seem to have an intuitive understanding of the distinction between inflection and derivation, but the objective criteria behind this intuition have proved difficult to find. Katamba (1993:205) observes that there is in practice no unanimity among linguists in the classification of processes as inflectional or derivational. He affirms that even grammarians working on the same language may not agree as to which processes are to be treated as inflectional and which ones are to be regarded as derivational. Across languages, there can even be greater confusion.

Jespersen (1924:42) remarks that a distinction between inflection and derivation is bound to be artificial in some cases. He cites examples with French where the application of the same process yields different results. For instance, the application of double 'n' plus 'e' (i.e. 'nne') to *bon* yields *bonne* which is regarded as inflectional and the application of the same double 'n' plus 'e' to *paysan* yields *paysanne* which is regarded as derivational in the language. Jespersen wonders how the same formal and semantic modification can yield different results. It must, however, be pointed out that the two operands (i.e. the bases to which the new formatives are added) belong to different morphological classes.

Bybee (1985:81) describes the distinction between inflection and derivation as the most persistent undefinables in morphology. He claims that the basis of their distinction is the relevance of morphological categories. According to Bybee, all morphological categories must be high in relevance and the differences in the degrees of relevance yield the derivational/inflectional distinction as well as the hierarchical relations within the two broad types.

Following Bybee and Jespersen, Spencer (1991:9) opines that it is extremely difficult to draw the line between inflection and derivation in such a way that it gives sensible answers for all languages.

Though linguists have argued on the difficulty of distinguishing between inflection and derivation, there have been ample suggestions in the literature of how inflection could be distinguished from derivation. In distinguishing inflection from derivation, for instance, Katamba (1993:205) says that Greenberg (1954) proposes obligatoriness, productivity, and syntactic motivation as criteria for characterizing inflection. Katamba explains that inflection occurs at different points in a sentence and that syntax imposes obligatory choices from a menu of affixes.

Bybee (1985:81) upholds this view of obligatoriness as the most successful criterion for distinguishing inflection from derivation because he argues that obligatory categories force certain choices upon the speaker. He maintains that derivational morphology is transitional between lexical and inflectional expression and that the differences that can be observed between inflectional and derivational expression are just more prominent instances of the differences identifiable among inflectional categories.

Katamba (1993:207) challenges this view by saying that the criterion of obligatoriness cannot always successfully distinguish inflection from derivation because there are cases where syntactic well-formedness requires the selection of a form with a particular derivational suffix. The following constructions are illustrative:

1. Sabina gives an intelligent suggestion
2. Sabina suggests intelligently

In the above examples, we observe that to get a well-formed sentence as in (1) and (2), we must apply the derivational rule that suffixes '–ly' to the adjective *intelligent* and turns it into the adverb *intelligently*. Katamba argues that inflectional morphology deals with syntactically determined affixation processes, while derivational morphology is used to create new words. He describes some affixes as syntactically more pertinent than others. Citing example with the inflectional morpheme '–s,' in English, Katamba regards the inflectional affix as the more syntactically pertinent one because the morpheme –s is obligatory in verbs as it realizes in them the syntactically pertinent properties of third person present tense and singular number, but the derivational prefix, for example 'ex-' as in *ex-wife* which is not syntactically pertinent is not obligatory in nouns appearing in any sentence position.

Bauer (1989:22) discusses inflection/derivation in terms of commutability, close/open system, and large/small classes. He states that affixes which are members of large classes to which new items can be freely added are not inflectional, but those which are members of small classes to which it is impossible to add extra members are inflectional. With respect to open/close system, Bauer observes that inflection involves relatively few variables in a closed system. For instance, the category of number in English has only two values – singular and plural. With respect to derivation, Bauer (1989:26) defines derivation as the morphological process that results in the formation of new lexemes. He opines that derivation involves many variables in an open class, that it is characterized by low commutability with the word-form but that a few kinds of derivation are characterized by high commutability within the sentence form. Examples include feminine forms in '–ess' in English, diminutives and augmentatives in Italian.

Distinguishing derivation from inflection, Greenberg (1954) as recorded in Bybee (1985:81) defines derivational morpheme as:

> … morphemes which when in construction with a root morpheme establish a sequence which may always be substituted for some particular class of single morpheme in all instances without producing a change in the construction.

Greenberg cites English examples with such nouns as *duckling* which may be substituted for monomorphemic nouns as *duck, turkey, goose,* etc without changing the construction. Note that none of the constructions with *duck—*, etc, above requires the *–ling* suffix. With respect to inflection, Greenberg observes that being a bound non-root morpheme, the appearance of inflectional morpheme in a particular position is compulsory. For instance, in constructions like the following English progressives,

3. The boys are singing
4. The cat is mousing
5. The duckling is swimming

The progressive marker *–ing* in numbers (3), (4), and (5) cannot be substituted with any monomorphemic word without changing the construction entirely. If any of the progressive verbs above is replaced with a non-progressive verb, the sentence will be ungrammatical. An inflectional category is obligatorily marked any time a stem category to which it applies appears in a finite clause.

Matthews (1974:48) proposes that inflectional morphemes are those which are required by the syntax of the sentence. This proposal agrees with Katamba's view that describes inflectional affixes as more syntactically pertinent than others.

Bybee (1985:82) quotes Bloomfield (1933) as saying that inflection is characterized by a 'rigid parallelism of underlying and resultant forms'. That is to say that inflectional paradigms are highly structured sets of words with regular patterns. Bybee (1985:82) also records Bloomfield's (1933) and Nida's (1946) individual observations that derivational morphemes occur closer to the root than inflectional morphemes.

This observation confirms Spencer's (1997) and Eka's (2004) individual claims which state that inflectional affixes are attached more peripherally to the stem than are derivational ones. The reason, of course, being that the lexeme by derivational process should be present before a set of inflectional forms of it can apply.

Katamba (1993:209) quotes Anderson (1988a:167) as identifying four kinds of morphological properties/categories which are the characteristics of inflection. Such properties include: configurational properties, agreement properties, inherent properties, and phrasal properties.

2.3.1 Configurational Properties
The choice of a particular inflection is determined by the place occupied by a word in a syntactic configuration; that is, its position and function as a constituent of a phrase or some other syntactic structures.

Example:

- a noun object of a preceding preposition must receive accusative case marking.
- a direct object of a verb must be in the accusative case.
- a verb in a subordinate clause must have a special form such as the subjunctive mood.

2.3.2 Agreement Properties

These are determined by the characteristics of another word or words in the same construction. (Example, if an adjective modifies a singular noun, it must be assigned a singular affix whose form depends on the form of the affix in the noun it is modifying).

2.3.3 Inherent Properties

Inherent properties: the gender of a noun must be accessed by agreement rules. (Example, the gender of a French or German noun determines the gender of the adjective that modifies it).

2.3.4 Phrasal Properties

Phrasal properties belong to an entire syntactic phrase, but are morphologically realized in one of the words of that phrase. (Example, genitive -'s in English phrases like *The Mayor of Lancaster's limousine* where, although the mayor is the possessor of the limousine, the —'s inflection is attached to *Lancaster*).

Spencer (1997:193) describes the nature of inflectional morphology as one of the most problematic areas of morphological theory, stating that it is the one on which there are perhaps more disagreements than any other aspect. He regards inflection as a change in the grammatical or morphosyntactic form of a word or lexeme as opposed to derivation which is the formation of a new lexeme from another lexeme. Spencer discusses the notions associated with inflectional morphology under morphological class and paradigm. Morphological class, according to Spencer, is a phenomenon that is common in languages that exhibit rich inflection. In such languages, the words of a given syntactic class do not have the same inflection – they are rather arranged into more or less arbitrary groupings that are associated with different sets of inflection.

Spencer observes that inflectional morphology often organizes itself into paradigms. He describes a paradigm as a set of all the inflected forms which an individual word assumes. A paradigm is, according to Crystal (1997:277), a set of grammatically conditioned forms all derived from a single root or stem.

Scholars, including Robins (1964), Bybee (1985:82), Katamba (1993:47), and Ejele (1996:89), recognize two types of derivational morphemes – those that change the syntactic category of the word to which they apply and those that do not. In the case of verbs, change in syntactic category means the extent to which the meaning of the morpheme affects the description of the situation, and in the case of nouns, it means the extent to which the meaning of the morpheme changes the referent of the noun.

Bybee (1985) argues that derivational processes that do not change syntactic category are characterized by large meaning changes while those that do change the syntactic category of a word make varying amounts of semantic change depending on how much semantic content they contribute along with the category change.

2.4 The Nature of Words

Many linguists including Hockett (1958:167), Lyons (1979:200), Bloomfield (1933), Crystal (1997:419) have defined words in different ways. For instance, Bloomfield (1933) defines a word as a minimum free form. Hockett (1958) defines a word as any segment of a sentence bounded by successive points at which pausing is possible, and Lyons (1979:200) defines a word semantically as the union of a particular meaning with a particular complex of sounds capable of a particular grammatical employment. A speech community imposes meaning onto words in the language. It is conventionally at the disposal of the speech community to adopt certain words and meanings as they are. The concept *book*, for instance, is conventionally accepted as the name of book in the English language. The same book is conventionally accepted as *livre* and *akwụkwọ* in the French and Igbo languages, respectively.

The internal structure of words is rule-governed (Fromkin and Rodman 1998:69). Newmeyer states that the principles governing the internal structure of words are quite different from those that determine the internal structure of phrases. This is because the lexical rules are local in the sense that they can only refer to materials with the subcategorization frame of a single item. Syntactic rules, on the other hand, can relate positions not within a single item's subcategorization frame. The rules for the internal structure of words are distinct in type (as well as in language particular content) from rules that organize words into phrases and larger constructions. This rule accounts for the fixed order of the occurrence of morphemes. A word is therefore not just a simple sequence of morphemes, but has a hierarchical structure.

Linguists, including Matthews (1974) and Aronoff (1976), regard words as the minimal unit of meaning, but Tomori (1977) and Katamba (1993) describe morphemes, not words, as the minimal or smallest unit of meaning and grammar.

2.5 Illustrations of Affixation Process Using Different Languages

Affixation processes vary from one language to another. The type also varies from one language to another. In some languages, prefixation is predominant, while in others, it is suffixation, interfixation, infixation, or circumfixation that dominates. Superfixation/suprafixation is attested to in all tonal languages, and most African languages are tonal languages. Fromkin and Rodman (1998:71) illustrate extensively the affixation processes drawing examples from many languages spoken in different parts of the world. We shall elicit from their examples and demonstrate the affixation processes in some of the world's languages.

2.5.1 Number

In Zapotec, a language spoken in Oaxaca, Mexico, the plural morpheme *ka-* is prefixed to a noun to change it to plural, as in the following examples:

6. zigi *chin*   kazigi *chins*
7. zike *shoulder* kazike *shoulders*
8. diaga *ear*   kadiaga *ears*

(cf. Fromkin and Rodman 1998:71).

Kari (2004:240) states that in Degema, a Delta Edoid language spoken in Rivers state, number is marked by a set of vowel prefixes attached before the noun stem. He adds that the stem of nouns making the singular/plural distinction must be bound, and can never occur without a prefix. Kari claims that the prefix alternation in the formation of nouns in Degema is a highly productive process, and that the number-marking prefixes agree in expandedness or non-expandedness with the vowels of the noun stem, depending on the quality of the vowels of the noun stem.

Ndimele (1999:54) illustrates, with examples derived from the English language, the different allomorphs of the same plural morpheme *s*. {Iz, z, s} being phonologically conditioned. This morpheme is suffixed to a noun to form its plural (this is the regular plural formation in the language). The following examples show the plural forms and their variants/realizations in English:

	Singular	*Plural*
A	school /skuːl/	schools /skuːlz/
B	boy /bɔːɪ/	boys /bɔːɪz/
C	town /taʊn/	towns /taʊnz/
D	store /stɔː/	stores /stɔːz/
E	church /tʃəːtʃ/	churches /tʃəːtʃɪz/
F	bucket /bʌkit/	buckets /bʌkits/

Table 2-I Variants of the plural morphemes

The above are different phonetic realizations of the same plural morphemes in English. French also marks its plural with the morpheme 's'; it differs, however, from the English plural in that, while the English plural morpheme is suffixed only to nouns, the French plural morpheme 's' is, according to Mitterand (1969:10), suffixed to nouns, determinants, adjectives, and past participles of verbs, as in the following examples:

9. Le garçon est gentil *singular*
   Les garçons sont gentils *plural*
   The (pl) boys are pleasant *plural*
   Le grand verre est cassé *singular*
   Les grands verres sont cassés *plural*
   The (pl) big(pl) glasses(pl) are broken *plural*

2.5.2 Negation
In French, according to Bled (1954:162), negation is formed regularly by flanking the verb with negative adverbial locutions, as in:

10. ne……pas   *not*
11. ne……plus   *no more*
12. ne……jamais   *never*

13. ne……guere	*scarcely* etc.	
14. Ne mange pas	*Don't eat*	
15. Ne regarde jamais	*Never look*	
16. N'écrit plus	*Write no more*	

2.5.3 Nominal Derivation

The nominal derivation in Turkish, a language spoken in Turkey was described by Fromkin and Rodman (1998:71). They state that nominals are derived from the verbs by the insertion of the suffix '-ak' to the verb roots, as in the following examples:

17. dur	*to stop*	dur + ak	*stopping place*
18. bat	*to sink*	bat + ak	*sinking place*

2.5.4 Verbal Derivative
2.5.4.1 Infix

In Bontoc, a language spoken in the Phillipines, as reported by Fromkin and Rodman (1998:71), the verb is derived from the noun or adjective by inserting the infix '-um-' after the first oral consonant of the noun or adjective, as shown in the examples below:

19. pusi	*poor*	pumusi	*to be poor*
20. ngitad	*dark*	ngumitad	*to be dark*

2.5.4.2 Interfix

Ndimele (1999:32) regards interfix as a very productive process of word derivation in the Igbo language because many dynamic and stative verbs lend themselves to it. He describes it as an affix which occurs between two identical or sometimes non-identical roots thereby interrupting the sequence of the two roots. The following are some examples:

21. ánú	*meat*	án*ų*màn*ų̀*	*mammal*
22. èkwú	*speak*	èkwúrèkwú	*talkativeness*

The 'interfix' in the above examples is *m* and *r*.

2.5.4.3 Circumfix

Ejele (1996:84) and Anagbọgụ (2001:102) identify circumfix in the Esan and Igbo languages respectively. Some of the examples cited by the two linguists are as follow:

The Esan language (Ejele 1996:84)

23. tue	*hot*	útuèmin	*hotness*
24. so	*shout*	úsòmin	*the shout*

The circumfixal frame in Esan is *u ... min*. The observation is that a nominalized form is produced in the language when the circumfix is added simultaneously at the beginning and at the end of the word.

Igbo language (Anagbọgụ 1990:93)
25. esimụncha *act of making soap*
26. agbamụọsọ *act of running*

Anagbọgụ gives the circumfixal frame in Igbo as *a/e ... mu* and argues that it is very productive in the Igbo language. Similarly, in the Malay language, and in Eleme (a kegboid language spoken in Rivers State, Nigeria), the discontinuous affixes *pē ... an* and *e ... e* respectively have been recognized as circumfixes in the formation of abstract nouns and infinitive verb forms in the languages. Ndimele (1999:33ff) gives examples of abstract nouns and infinitive verb forms as cited by Allerton (1979:220) and Alesi (1998:26) in the aforementioned languages. For instance, in Eleme, the following derivatives have been recorded:

	Base Form	*Derived Form*
A	sì *go*	èsíè *to go*
B	jù *come*	èjúè *to come*
C	lì *bury*	èlíè *to bury*
D	jà *buy*	èjáè *to buy*

Table 2-II Circumfixes in Eleme

From the foregoing examples, we however observe that the morphological circumfixal frame (or paradigm) in Esan and Eleme languages present identical morphological patterns which can be symbolized as Y-b-Z, where:

- *Y represents the first part of the discontinuous morpheme*
- *b represents the base or the verb root*
- *Z represents the second part of the discontinuous morpheme* as in the following examples:

Esan: u ... (b) ... min ex: tue (base): u-tue-min *hotness*
$$\text{base}$$
$$\text{hot}$$

Eleme: e ... (b) ... e ex: si (base): e-si-e *to go*
$$\text{base}$$
$$\text{go}$$

In Igbo, the morphological circumfixal framework, though comparable to those of Esan and Eleme, presents some peculiarities in the sense that the circumfix requires a verbal complement in order to be complete and meaningful and the vocalic morpheme of the base harmonizes with it (the base) which can be symbolized as Y-b-Z + complement, where

- Y = *harmonizing vocalic morpheme (first part)*
- b = *base or verb root*
- Z = *second part of the discontinuous morpheme*
- compl = *complement*

Examples:

    sí (cook)   è-sí-mú(or m) + ńní
    (base)   food

    zà (sweep)   à-zà-mụ̀(or m) + ụ́nọ̀
    (base)   house

It is noteworthy that circumfixation can be used to derive nominals in Igbo, abstract nouns in Esan, and infinitives in Eleme.

Onukawa (1999:121) rejects the circumfixal frame posited by Anagbogu (1990) and argues that the constituents are separate derivational elements. He states that the initial syllabics in the Igbo circumfixal derivatives are derivational prefixes while the "m" is a derivational suffix. This is an issue which needs further investigation.

2.5.4.4 Super/suprafix

Ndimele (1999:35) describes superfix/suprafix as an affix which is marked over syllables in languages where they exist. He states that superfix comes in the form of tones or stress marks placed over words. For instance, in English, superfix is expressed as stress, while in tone languages, it is expressed as tones. It provokes a meaning difference between segmentally identical words. The superfix expressed in the form of stress can be seen in the following English words:

27. 'contest *noun*   con'test *verb*
28. 'import *noun*   im'port *verb* etc.

In the Igbo language, the superfix can be expressed as follows:

29. àkwà *bed*   ọ̀kẹ̀ *a share*
30. ákwá *cry*   ọ́kẹ́ *male*
31. ákwà *cloth*   ọ́kẹ̀ '*boundary*
32. àkwá *egg*   ọ̀kẹ́ *rat*

Essien (1990:10ff) explains the various derivational functions of suffixes in Ibibio. He states that some suffixes are verb-forming as different from noun-forming, for instance, in Ibibio, the *nucleus* is either CVC or CV and to this, either a vowel or a nasal can be prefixed to derive a noun, or a suffix can be added to derive a verb. Boyd (1989:205) states that suffixation is essentially derivational in the Ubangi sub-family of Adamawa-Ubangi. Noss (1991) argues that suffixation is responsible for the derivation of the two categories of derived nouns in Gbaya.

2.6 Processes of affixation in Igbo

Before considering affixation in Igbo, effort will be made to examine the status of the Igbo verb because the verb is an indispensable element in affixation in the language and, according to Igwe and Green (1963:64): "The verb is distinguished formally from all the other parts of speech by the fact that it is the only one in which an inflectional affix is found".

Emenanjo (1975:52) defines the Igbo verb, not only as the constituent that immediately precedes the complement in the VP, but also as the only form class which requires a complement to be complete and meaningful. He gives the following distinctive features of the Igbo verb:

* The Igbo verb has two or more of the following verbal derivatives, namely: the infinitive; the participle; the Bound Cognate Noun (BCN), and the gerund.
* It can be nominalized.
* It can be emphasized by the different types of nominals in the surface adverbial slot: the BCN, the ideophones, etc.
* It selects its subject and its object.

At this juncture, it is pertinent to state that there is an internal constraint which governs the selection of subject and its object in the Ọnịcha dialect of Igbo, as we shall see ahead. Speaking further on the importance and indispensability of verbs in Igbo, Emenanjo (1983:43) states:

> The verb is the only form class from which useful plethora of cognate lexical items or varying morphological structure and equally of varying syntactic behaviour have been derived and can still be derived, at least for a good majority of them.

Onukawa (2002:44) rejects the view that verb roots are the fundamental source of derivation in diachronic Igbo. He says rather that derivations in diachronic Igbo were sourced from *core* or *radical elements*. These were, according to him, the *nominalizing radical elements* (ie those that derive the nominals) and the *verbalizing radicals* (ie those that derive the verbals). These have reanalyzed (semantically) to other elements in the language including what is referred to as *verb roots* in synchronic Igbo.

Onukawa gives the following examples for derivation of nominals:

CV Nominalizing Radical Element	Reanalyzed (Extant) Verb Root	Derived Nominal
Bù	-bù *sing*	ábù̩ (á-bù̩) *a song*
Gwù	-gwù *play*	égwú (é-gwú) *a play*
Wé	-wé *be angry*	íwé (í-wé) *anger*

Jé	-jé *walk*	íjè (í-jè) *a walk*
Tó	-tó *grow*	ùtó (ù-tó) *growth*
Chè	-chè *think*	úchè (ú-chè) *thought*
Kwú	-kwú *speak*	ókwú (ó-kwú) *speech*
Dó	-dó *be in order*	ùdó (ù-dó) *peace*

He gives the following examples for the derivation of verbals:

Verbalizing Radical Elements	**Derived Verbal Infinitive**
* Bà	ịbà (í-bà) *to enter*
* Tọ́	í'tó (í-tô) *to grow*
* Kọ́	ị'kọ́ (ị-kọ́) *to tell*
* Dẹ́	ị'dẹ́ (ị-dẹ́) *to write*
* Kwú	í'kwú (í-kwú) *to speak*
* Bí	í'bí (í-bí) *to live in*

Verbalizing Radicals and the Derivation of Simple Participles:

CV Verbalizing Radical Element	**Derived Verbal (Simple Participle**
* Bà	abà (a-ba) *entering*
* To	èto (è-to) *growing*
* Kọ	àkọ (à-kọ) *telling*
* De	èdo (e-de) *writing*
* Le	èle (è-le) *looking*

Igwe and Green (1963) observe that the Igbo verb is characterized by great complexity of detail, but by simplicity and symmetry of system. Okonkwo (1974:23) describes the Igbo verb root as the nucleus or permanent stump on which prefixes and suffixes are attached in order to get the different forms of the verb. Emenanjo (1975:52) affirms that the verbal system in general and in particular the verbs are the only source in the Igbo language for deriving new words. This opinion is shared by many other scholars, including Green and Igwe (1963), Abraham (1967), Williamson (1972), Igwe (1977), and Nwachukwu (1983). Nwachukwu (1983:18) observes that morphological processes in the Igbo language are unidirectional, always starting from the simple CV-stem and giving rise to other lexical categories but never reversible. Nwachukwu's observation also confirms Igbo as a verb language, a phenomenon corroborated by Ndimele (2001). Ward (1936), as recorded in Welmers (1973:330) distinguishes between a compound verb and a *meaning suffix*. She states that a compound verb is a base consisting of two verb roots, each of which occurs independently as a monosyllabic verb base. A *meaning suffix* she describes as a morpheme which appears in second position in a two-syllable verb base, but which does not occur independently as a monosyllabic verb base; yet which adds something to the meaning of the preceding root.

2.6.1 Classification of Igbo Verbs

Scholars, including Emenanjo (1978:140), Nwachukwu (1983:28) and Ndimele (1999:95), group Igbo verbs into two major classes. Emenanjo uses the terms *active* and *stative* in his classification; Nwachukwu applies the terms *stative* and *non-stative*, while Ndimele prefers the terms *dynamic* and *stative* verbs. We shall adopt Emenanjo's terminology in this work because it is easily understood and more straight forward.

2.6.1.1 Active Verb

Emenanjo (1978:140) describes active verbs as those which are used for expressing action or activity. He attributes the following qualities to them:

- they can be used in the imperative
- they express past time meaning in the indicative constructions
- they can immediately be followed by the directional extensional suffix =te/=ta *motion towards*; *for, from*, in a literal sense.

With active verbs, the subject of the construction is the agent which acts upon or affects something else.

2.6.1.2 Stative Verb

Emenanjo (1975:66) defines stative verbs as those used for expressing qualities and states as well as existential notions of beings. He states that the Igbo stative verbs are used for expressing adjectival notions and affirms that four out of the few adjectives recognized in Igbo are derived from stative verbs. Similarly, Nwachukwu (1983:29) describes stative verbs as those verbs which refer, not to an activity, but to a state or condition. He groups them into two inflectional groups:

- those that take –rV suffix
- those that do not take –rV suffix

He observes that the majority of the stative verbs in Igbo are characterized by their taking –rV suffix to express a present meaning. The co-occurrence of the –rV suffix with verb forms that express present meaning was used to argue a case for the non-relevance of tense in Igbo. Welmers (1973:360) states that stative verbs are used in Ọnịcha to express descriptive meaning, while they are used in the factative sense in the Central Igbo dialect. He gives the following examples in both the Ọnịcha and the Central Igbo dialects:

ỌNỊCHA DIALECT			CENTRAL IGBO DIALECT		
Ó	nwèè̩	é'gó	Ó	nwèrè	é'gó
He/she	possess	money	He/she	possess	money
He/she has money			He/she has money		

ỌNỊCHA DIALECT			CENTRAL IGBO DIALECT		
Ó	pèè̩	mpè̩	Ó	pèrè	mpé
He/she	be small	small	He/she	be small	small
He/she is small			He/she is small		
Ó	cò̩ò̩	ńní	Ó	cò̩rò̩	ńní
He/she	want	food	He/she	want	food
He/she wants food			He/she wants food		
Ọ́	tò̩	ùtó̩	Ọ́	tò̩rò̩	ùtó̩
It	be sweet	sweet	It	be sweet	sweet
It is sweet			It is sweet		

Table 2-III Welmers' examples of stative verb uses in Ọnịcha and Central Igbo

From the foregoing examples, we observe that the realizations in the two dialects are identical whether it is description or factative expression.

Nwachukwu (1983:67) observes that constructions with the –rV non-time suffix can also be expressed in the past form in some dialects. He gives the following examples with the Central Igbo dialect:

Òbí	nwèèrè	é'gó
Obi	vb.rt-*ext.suff*-FT	money
Obi used to have money		
Àdá bùùrù		íbù
Ada vb.rt-*ext.suff*-FT		fatness
Ada used to be fat		

Table 2-IV Nwachukwu's examples of rV non-time suffix in the Central Igbo Dialect

In the Ọnịcha dialect of Igbo, the examples above will be realized as:

Òbí nwè̩*bù*lù	é'gó
Obi vb.rt-*ext.suff*-FTmoney	
have	
Obi used to have money	
Àdá bù*bù*lù	íbù
Ada vb.rt-*ext.suff*-FT	fatness
be fat	
Ada used to be fat	

Table 2-V The Ọnịcha Igbo realization of -rV non-time suffix

In some other Central Igbo dialects, it is not uncommon to hear realizations such as:

33. Òbí nwèbùrù é'gó
    Obi used to have money

34. Àdá bùbùrù íbù
    Ada used to be fat

2.7 Affixes as Important Elements of Derivation in Igbo
The study of affixation has been one of the major preoccupations of Igbo linguists and grammarians. Emenanjo (1972, 1982), Anagbọgụ (1990), Ndimele (1999), and Ngoesi (2000) identify prefixes, interfixes, circumfixes, supra/superfixes, and suffixes as affixes attested in the Igbo language. Emenanjo (1978:91) breaks down Igbo suffixes into inflectional and extensional types, while Nwachukwu (1983:61) divides affixes into inflectional and non-inflectional types. He groups derivational prepositional –rV suffixes and extensional suffixes under non-inflectional suffixes. Following Emenanjo and Nwachukwu, Nwigwe (1996:9) classifies affixes in Igbo morphology under the following headings:

- derivational
- inflectional
- extensional

Nwachukwu (1983:18) affirms that derivation in Igbo starts and ends with the simple CV-stem. He argues that Igbo dialects differ considerably in the number of derivatives that can originate from any given verb and that the Central dialects seem to be more prolific than the northern dialects to which Ọnịcha belongs. Nwachukwu attributes the low productivity of the northern dialects to their highly simplified phonology devoid of aspiration and nasalization.

2.7.1 Deverbatives
Ndimele (2001:38) uses the term *deverbatives* to denote nominals which are derived directly from verbs. Eke (1985:179) lists the following as characteristics and processes of derivations in Igbo:

i. The Igbo language, like English and many other languages achieve most of its derivative processes through affixation.
ii. The attachment of a derivative morpheme to a root or base may bring about a tonal modification in the derived word.
iii. The derivative morpheme attaches to the root according to the rules of vowel harmony.
iv. A great majority of the derivations in Igbo are noun-verb derivations.

Eke distinguishes total and partial reduplications from other derivatives that involve neither total nor partial reduplication. Such derivatives, he argues, express either:

- abstract qualities
- names of objects
-

He represents the process of total reduplication in Ohafia Igbo as OCV_1CV_2, where:

- O represents the derivative morpheme, which is realized either as 'Ọ' or 'O' according to vowel harmony.
- CV₁ represents the reduplicated verb root.
- CV₂ represents the verb root.

The same process of derivation through reduplication is applicable to Ọnịcha Igbo. Anagbọgụ (1990:42) distinguishes regular processes of nominalization from the irregular ones. He identifies seven forms of regular nominalization processes and states that they are highly productive in Igbo, while the irregular forms belong to the old formation which is no longer productive. We do not, however, adopt some of the examples given by Anagbọgụ, as they are not applicable to the Ọnịcha dialect.

2.7.2 Verbal Deverbatives

Emenanjo applies *verbals* as a general term for the three elements which feature in the Igbo verbal system. The three elements are:

- auxiliaries
- participles
- verbs

He states that these elements have two distinct types of grammatical behaviour which are peculiar to them and different from other grammatical categories in the language. The peculiar behaviour of the verbals are:

a) They alone take inflectional affixes – prefixes and suffixes.
b) They alone can be found in the verbal slot of the sentence as its only essential component.

The verb is the only part of speech that takes affixes (Emenanjo 1978:134). A verbal derivative is therefore, according to Emenanjo (1975:111), any word which is formed or derived from a verb by affixation or by reduplication. The affixes involved in the process of derivation may be derivational or inflectional which may in turn involve the use of prefixes or suffixes or both.

2.7.3 Derivational Morphology

Emenanjo (1976:27) states that certain derivational affixes in Igbo are conditioned by vowel harmony. For instance, the following derivational affixes obey the rules of vowel harmony:

a) the infinitive prefix i-/ị-
b) the derivational vowel prefix of the noun agent o-/ọ
c) the affix involved in the formation of verbal nouns or gerunds.

Emenanjo (1978:215) observes that most Igbo prefixes are derivational, while suffixes are mostly involved in extensional and inflectional morphology though some suffixes are also involved in union with prefixes to achieve derivation. Onukawa (2000:57) refers to the derivation that involves prefixation and reduplication as the *deverbative reduplicated nouns*. He points out that these nouns resemble the simple gerundive nominals from the morphological point of view but differ from them from the semantic notion. Onukawa also distinguishes the deverbative reduplicated nouns from what he calls the *denominal reduplicated nouns*. He says that the former has a verbal base, while the latter has a nominal base. But the terminology *denominal reduplicated noun*, applied by Onukawa to *noun-noun reduplicated derivatives* appears confusing. This is because, as the name denominal implies, when a noun is denominalized and reduplicated, the derivative ceases to be a nominal unless another process is applied to renominalize it.

Comparing the synthetic compound and the nominal compound in Igbo, Anagbọgụ (2000:51) observes that the synthetic compound formation in Igbo is a highly productive process and the meaning is very specific, even to a non-native speaker because of its verbal content.

Describing the derivation of gerundive nominals in Igbo, Onukawa (1992:91) states that they are derived from simple verb roots by the nominalization processes of reduplication, tone copying, and prefixation. He distinguishes between gerundive meaning and purpose meaning of the derivative. Onukawa (1995:266) rejects the view that nominals can be derived from sentences in Igbo. He argues that such nominals are deverbatives which are derived from verb roots and that the derivational processes involved are basically prefixation and suffixation. Commenting on the behaviour of tones in Igbo constructions, Emenanjo (1978:172) observes that the tone of vowel prefix in the negative indicative verb forms is conditioned by the NP. He states that when the NP is a singular pronoun, it bears a low tone and the first element of the verb stem bears a high tone. With other NPs, the tone on the prefix is high. The vowel suffix copies the inherent tone of the verb root.

2.7.4 Interfixation as a Derivational Process in Igbo
Frick (1978), as recorded by Emenanjo (1982), defines interfix as:

> ... affix which occurs between the verb root and the final suffix or occasionally between the verb root and the final vowel of the base form. They can never occur in the word final position. They are in form and function quite distinct from the suffixes. Whereas the suffixes are mutually exclusive, i.e. a verb can contain no more than one, several interfixes can occur together.

The above definition of interfix is applicable to Dghwede language spoken in Bornu State of Nigeria. With respect to the Igbo language, Emenanjo (1982:84) defines Igbo interfixes as morphemes which perform distinct derivational functions for deriving types of verbal derivatives from verbs or for deriving new nouns from nouns.

Ndimele (1999:32) also defines Igbo interfix as an affix which occurs between two identical or sometimes non-identical roots (i.e. an affix which interrupts the sequence of two roots). Emenanjo (1982:84) argues that Igbo clearly has affixes which qualify to be called interfixes in view of their distinct morphological position in the derivatives in which they are found. He gives the morphological structure of the verbal derivatives containing interfixes as:

    prefix – verb root – interfix – prefix – verb root.

This morphological structure is for verb-base interfixation. Since interfixes are also attested in nominal derivations which do not require prefix to achieve the derivation, the morphological structure of nominal derivatives containing interfixes will be represented as:

    Noun – Interfix – Noun

Emenanjo remarks that in words derived through interfixation in Igbo, there is a neat, symmetrical arrangement between the two components linked by the interfix. The derivation may or may not cause tonal changes in the derived words.

2.7.5 Suffixation as Part of the Derivational Process in Ọnịcha

As has been mentioned earlier in this work, prefixes and interfixes can each achieve derivational processes in Igbo without combining with other affixes. In the case of suffixes, they can achieve derivational processes alone but as class-maintaining extensional suffixes. Kelly (1954:17) describes verb-suffixes in Igbo as devices for expressing complete ideas. Emenanjo (1973:97) describes a suffix as any bound but optional element which primarily occurs on the verb in the verbal slot. This characteristic of occurring primarily and exclusively with verbs in the verbal slot distinguishes suffixes from enclitics which attach to verbs as well as to nouns. Nwachukwu (1983:65) describes Igbo suffixes as the major tense/aspect markers in both Central Igbo and other dialects. He recognizes one tense in Igbo – the simple past, marked by the =rV time suffix. Emenanjo (1978:90) and Uwalaka (1997:73) remark that suffixes feature so consistently and so prominently in Igbo sentence/grammar that they deserve to be called a part of speech. Most discussions on the Igbo suffixes in popular Igbo grammar books tend to suggest that Igbo suffixes are either inflectional or extensional. Supporting Nwachukwu's recognition of one tense marked by =rV time suffix in Igbo, this book observes that aspect is marked in the following way in Ọnịcha:

- The imperfective constructions express:

    o present meaning where examples show as expressions of either habitual or progressive actions.
    o the future meaning which, apart from expressing prospective actions, expresses some modal implications depending on whether the perfective suffix =go is attached to the verb or not.

- The *perfective constructions* express past actions with present relevance and they are formed with the perfective suffix =go.
- The *unfulfilled perfective constructions* express actions which ought to have taken place before the moment of speaking; they are formed with the unfulfilled marker =ka. They express hypothetical and other modal meanings.

We agree with the views that consider grammatical and non-grammatical suffixes.

The =rV Suffix
Onukawa (1994:83) broadly classes the =rV suffixes into:

- Derivational =rV suffixes
- Non-derivational =rV suffixes

According to his classification, the derivational class comprises the derivational =rV suffixes, while the non-derivational class is made up of the inflectional =rV suffixes and the extensional =rV suffixes.

Uwalaka (1997:74) groups the =rV inflectional suffixes into:

- =rV stative/assertive/present
- =rV past time suffix

She says that the =rV stative present suffix co-occurs with a sub-class of stative verbs, and expresses a present time meaning, while the =rV past suffix is found with the past tense forms.

Onukawa describes the suffix =bu *used to* as an inflectional suffix. We do not share the views of Onukawa because, firstly, in the Ọnịcha dialect of Igbo, =bu indicates anteriority (a past time previous to the past of the discussion denoted by =lu/-lụ). Secondly, the =lu/-lụ is an inflectional suffix which can co-occur with =bu, and since two inflectional suffixes cannot co-occur in the same word, =bu can therefore be anything but an inflectional suffix.

Emenanjo (1978:146; 1983:46) describes some of the derivatives realized through the processes of prefixation and suffixation as diachronic morphology, and says that they belong to a closed system which is no longer productive. He gives the structural patterns of such derivatives as:

$V_1 - VR - V_2$

Where:

- V₁ is any vowel prefix
- VR is any verb root
- V₂ is the vowel of the verb root, which can be referred to as suffix.

Here are some of his examples:

PREFIX	VERB ROOT	SUFFIX
A	gụ	ụ
A	gbọ	ọ
U	ze	Le
U	ghe	Le
ẹ	kpẹ	lẹ

Table 2-VI Process of derivation through prefixation and suffixation

But Nwachukwu argues that some of the above words classed by Emenanjo as diachronic derivatives are not derived from verbs but are rather inherent complements of which the nominal complement and verbal must co-occur as one entity. In the case of Ọnịcha Igbo variety, some of the roots are not necessarily diachronic, and some do not only take their inherent complements because they can combine with other non-cognate noun complements to give other meanings. For instance, the verb roots gụ, gbọ, kpe, can be cognate only in the context of agụụ, *hunger*, agboọ, *vomit*, and ikpe *judge*. They can also co-occur in some other contexts with other noun complements as in:

VERB ROOT + COMPLEMENT	GLOSS	VERB ROOT + COMPLEMENT	GLOSS
gụ́ ọ́'nụ̀	Count	gbọ́ ùfụ́fụ̀	Foam
gụ́ 'jí	pick yam	gbọ́ ùjá	Bark
gụ́ í'sí	deliberate/reflect	gbọ́ ńní 'éwú	fetch fodder
kpẹ́ 'ẹ́kpẹ́lẹ́	Pray	ghẹ́ 'ḿmanụ́	fry oil
kpẹ́ í'kpé	Judge	ghẹ́ àzụ́	fry fish
		ghẹ́ 'jí	fry yam

Table 2-VII Some other co-occurrences of –rV suffixes

2.7.6 Inflectional Affixes

Nwachukwu (1983:61) defines inflection as changes in the internal structure of a word which determine its grammatical or syntactic function. He states that an affix is regarded as inflectional if it is an obligatory element of the verb form; that is, it needs to be present in a verb-form before it can express the appropriate time meaning.

Quoting Winston (1973), Nwachukwu remarks that the idea of polarity stems from the fact that Igbo verb inflection falls into two polar opposites or, what Green and Igwe (1963) describe as divisions – the Negative and Afirmative divisions.

Emenanjo (1978:91) observes that the Igbo inflectional suffixes function with the inflectional verbal vowel prefix, auxiliaries, and the syntactic tone patterns to mark the different aspects and verb forms. He remarks that certain suffixes can function without other elements like auxiliaries and tonal morpehemes to distinguish sentence types or verbal constructions. Emenanjo classes such suffixes as inflectional, e.g.:

i. the harmonizing open vowel suffix which is used in:

  a. the imperative and the hortative, which are realized as –a/-ẹ when the verb stem ends in any of the vowels ị, a, ọ, ụ, ẹ
  b. -e when the verb stem ends in any of the vowels i, e, o, u

ii. the optional perfective suffix –go
iii. the negative suffix used in non-imperative verb forms –rọ/-rọọ
iv. the negative imperative suffix –na/-naà
v. the harmonizing optional indicative suffix –li/-lị; -lu/-lụ; used thus:

  a. li when the verb stem ends in i
  b. lị when the verb stem ends in ị
  c. lu when the verb stem ends in u
  d. lụ when the verb stem ends in ụ

Emenanjo argues that the Igbo inflectional suffixes are mutually exclusive because of the syntactic function they perform in marking distinctive verb forms. He (1976:82) observes that each inflectional suffix marks a particular aspect or verb form, and is an essential and integral part of its underlying verb form even when the suffix is optionally deleted in the surface form. He cites examples of some indicative affirmative constructions where the inflectional –LV suffixes are optional or deleted on the surface structure, and yet the sentences are grammatical and meaningful. Emenanjo, however, remarks that there are considerable number of examples in which the –LV could be omitted in the surface structure. He concludes by saying that other inflectional suffixes are obligatory in the underlying structure, but optional in the surface structure. Each inflectional suffix is, therefore, part and parcel of its appropriate aspect and verb form.

2.7.7 Extensional Suffixes
The extensional suffix is defined by Emenanjo (1978:97) as:

> a term used in African linguistics for referring to elements, usually affixes, which function principally as meaning-modifiers i.e. extending the meaning of the word with which they are used.

From the above definition, the extensional suffixes form part of the suffixes which Kurylowicz (1936), Chafe (1970), and Emenanjo (1975) lump together under the term *lexical suffixes* because they argue that lexical suffixes are those with semantic values or with a relatively high degree of information content. Carrell (1970) refers to extensional suffixes as *meaning modifying suffixes* (MMS). Quoting Green (1964), Emenanjo (1982:143) states that apart from extending the meaning of verb roots, extensional suffixes in Igbo create stylistic effect, give statement force to verb forms, and also distinguish homonymous forms. Kari (1995:150) discusses extensional suffixes in Degema under class-maintaining type of derivational affixes. Ndimele (2003:37) uses the term *verbal extension* for extensional suffixes which alter the cognitive meaning of the verb root to which they are attached – without changing the part of speech of the word. He argues that the majority of Echie suffixes belong to the class of verbal extensions, and that they are useful means of overcoming the problem created by the dearth of free form prepositions in Echie. The prepositional functions of extensional suffixes in Echie, as recorded by Ndimele, are also applicable to Ọnịcha Igbo. Some Igbo analysts have, sometimes, applied different terms to differentiate the extensional suffix from the inflectional suffix. For instance, Nwachukwu (1976) describes extensional suffix as *benefactive*. Later Nwachukwu (1983) applies the term *prepositional suffix* to denote the suffix that expresses the notion *on behalf of...* or *for the benefit of...*. Following Welmers (1970a), Emenanjo (1978) uses the term *applicative* to refer to the extensional suffix which expresses the notion *on behalf of...* or *for the benefit of...*.

From the definitions and descriptions of different linguists of the term *extensional suffix*, we understand the term to mean a collective name given to all the affixes (apart from the inflectional) that extend the cognitive meaning of the verb root. Each of these suffixes has its particular function, but whatever function it performs is secondary or additional to the notion expressed by the verb to which it is attached. For instance, the terms *benefactive*, *applicative*, or *prepositional* express the prepositional notion. All other extensional suffixes in the language have each a particular notion attached to it. The extensional suffixes in Igbo are so many and cannot all be easily captured because each dialect has its own way of expressing these notions. There are, however, many of them that are used in the same way and are therefore commonly used in many Igbo dialects.

Chapter 3

Morpho-syntactic Features of inflectional affixes

1. Introduction

This chapter discusses the morpho-syntactic analysis of inflectional affixes in the Ọnịcha dialect of Igbo. An inflectional affix indicates grammatical relationship in the root or base of the word to which it is attached. The chapter is concluded by providing a recapitulatory table of inflectional verbal affixes in Ọnịcha Igbo.

Crystal (1997:195) defines inflection as a term used in morphology to refer to one of the two main categories or processes of word formation. An inflectional morpheme is an affix that is added to the root or stem of a word to indicate grammatical relationships (e.g. tense, aspect, number) (Yul-Ifode 2005: 308). Inflectional affixes give variants of an already existing word without forming new words. They are selected for syntactic reasons.

Nouns in Igbo are generally not inflected for tense, gender, or number, but quite a few nouns in the Ọnịcha dialect of Igbo are inflected for number. They form their plural by changing the singular vowel prefix into a plural one.

For example: o-/ọ- → i-/ị-. Examples include:

	SINGULAR		PLURAL	
A	ókènyè	*Adult*	ikènyè	*Adults*
B	òkólóbìà	*young man*	ikólóbìà	*young men*
C	Òkpòró	*Woman*	ikpòró	*young women*
D	Ókèì	*Man*	Ìkèì	*Men*

Table 3-I Plural formations in nouns in Ọnịcha

The above inflectional marking on nouns is peculiar to the few kinship nouns in Ọnịcha. Apart from the above examples, inflection in Ọnịcha Igbo affects only the verbs. The morpho-syntactic and semantic characteristics of inflectional affixes in Ọnịcha will be treated under the following headings:

- Inflectional affixes in indicative constructions (affirmative and negative)
- Inflectional affixes in imperative constructions (affirmative and negative)
- Inflectional affixes in imperfective constructions (present, present progressive, future prospective)
- Inflectional affixes in perfective constructions (present, past, future)
- Inflectional affixes in unfulfilled perfective constructions (affirmative and negative).

3.1 Inflectional Affixes in Indicative Constructions

Indicative, as defined by Crystal (1997:194), refers to verb forms or sentence/clause types used in the expression of statements and questions. we shall use the term 'indicative' to stand for what many linguists variously refer to as Aorist/indefinite by Spencer (1982); Ra-suffix by Ward (1935); Subject Verb form by Green and Igwe (1963); factative and stative by Welmers and Welmers (1968); past tense and state form by Abraham (1968); Ogbalu (1972); Okonkwo (1974); and indicative by Emenanjo (1978) (Source: Emenanjo 1978:170) The indicative construction may be affirmative or negative. In the Ọnịcha dialect of Igbo, the indicative affirmative is formed by affixing the indicative marker =LV (in the Central Igbo and some other Igbo dialects, it is realized as =rV) to the verb root. The factative suffix is a tense indicative which is not restricted to only verbs of activity, but also to stative verbs. When it co-occurs with active verbs, it expresses a simple past meaning which we shall represent as *FT*, but when it co-occurs with stative verbs, it expresses a timeless meaning or present state of being and we shall represent it as *ST*. In the Central Igbo dialect, the indicative marker or factative copies the features of the preceding syllable, but in the Ọnịcha dialect, it takes the harmonizing vowel of the verb root.

3.1.1 Inflectional Affixes in the Indicative Affirmative Constructions

1	Úchè sùlù ákwà Uche vb-LV cloth wash-FT Uche washed cloth
2	Fá jèlù áfịá They vb-LV market go-FT They went to market
3	Ó zàlù únọ̀ He/she vb-LV house sweep-FT He/she swept the house
4	Íbè bùlù íbù Ibe vb-LV fat be fat-ST Ibe is fat
5	Àdá màlù ḿ'má Ada vb-LV beauty be fine-ST Ada is beautiful
6	Ó tòlù ógónógó He/she vb-LV tallness be tall-ST He/she is tall

Table 3-II Affirmative indicative constructions in Ọnịcha

Affixation and Auxiliaries in Igbo 39

Sentences (1)-(3) express simple past actions because of the nature of the verbs. The verbs in the constructions are active/dynamic verbs. In such constructions, the objects of (1) and (3) are patients, while the object of sentence (2) is the goal. Sentences (4)-(6), on the other hand, express the non-past actions or the present state of being of the subjects. The explanation is that the verbs in the sentences (4)-(6) are stative verbs. The verbs in such constructions can be described as verbs of aesthetics or value judgment.

3.1.1a Vowel Realization

There are vowel harmony restrictions with the indicative suffixes, as shown in the following chart:

VOWEL OF VERB ROOT	SUFFIX
a, ẹ, ọ, ụ	lụ
u, o	Lu
I	Li
ị	lị

Table 3-III Indicative Suffixes and Combinations in Ọnịcha

The above can be re-expressed as below:

- i ⟶ li
- ị ⟶ lị
- ẹ ⟶ lụ
- a ⟶ lụ
- ọ ⟶ lụ
- ụ ⟶ lụ
- o ⟶ lu
- u ⟶ lu

The above are the possible co-occurrence of vowels and the inflectional suffixes in the indicative construction in Ọnịcha Igbo. The vowel of -LV suffix harmonizes with the vowel of the verb root, but does not copy it as is the case with the =rV equivalent in the Central Igbo dialect.

3.1.1b Tonal Realization

The tones of the verbs and those of indicative suffixes are low tones. The verb complements maintain their inherent tones.

3.1.1.1 =LV Benefactive

We shall discuss the functions of =LV suffixes as benefactive, applicative, or prepositions, as different linguists refer to them.

The =LV suffix, apart from expressing the simple past actions with active/dynamic verbs and timeless meaning with stative verbs, can play a prepositional, benefactive, or applicative role with certain verb forms. Following Igwe and Green (1964:21), we talk of –la (time) and –la (non-time) suffixes. When both are used together in the same sentence construction, there is a deletion of the consonant 'l' which causes two identical vowels to occur together. This makes for articulatory economy. As an illustration, we shall use examples to demonstrate the co-occurrence of the suffixes.

7	Úchè	sì*lì*lì̀	m̀	ńní
	Uche	vb-*LV*-<u>prep</u>	pro	food
		cook-*suff*-<u>suff</u>		
	Uche cooked for me/Uche cooked on my behalf			
8	Fá	jè*lù*lù̀	yà	áfíá
	They	vb-*LV*-<u>prep</u>	pro	market
		go-*suff*-<u>suff</u>		
	They went to market for him/her/They went to market on his\her behalf			
9	Ó	zà*lù*lù̀	fà	únò̩
	He/she	vb-*LV*-<u>prep</u>	pro	house
		sweep-*suff*-<u>suff</u>		
	He/she swept the house for them/He/she swept the house on their behalf			

Table 3-IV Co-occurrence of the –La (time) and –La (non-time) suffix in Ọnịcha

The above realizations may not always be heard in normal discussions because the native speaker will not want to waste his/her time and energy articulating all the sounds (including redundant ones) in the construction. Naturally, language abhors waste. There is an element of articulatory economy in language use, so that examples (7)-(9) above may be regarded as deep structure realizations. In the surface structure, the realizations are as follows:

10. Úchè sììlì m̀ ńní   *Uche cooked for me*
11. Fá jèèlù̩ yà áfíá   *They went to market for him*
12. Ó zààlù̩ fà únò̩   *He/she swept the house for them*

What we may say for sentences (10)-(12) above is that when the benefactive suffix is added to the indicative construction, there is a deletion of the consonant part of the suffix leaving only the vowels which regressively assimilate all the features of the preceding vowel. The indirect object pronouns are the beneficiaries in the constructions. The above examples are realizations with active verbs. With stative verbs, we shall have the following realizations which may appear ambiguous thus:

13. Íbè bùùlù m̀ íbù   *Ibe is fat for me*
14. Àdá mààlù̩ m̀ ḿ'má   *Ada is beautiful for me*
15. Ó tòòlù m̀ ógónógó   *He/she is tall for me*

We observe from the above data that sentences (10)-(12) are well-formed (acceptable) in the Ọnịcha dialect, while (13)-(15) are grammatical but could also be used ironically to express the exact opposite meaning especially when extraordinary or unusual feelings are expressed. The reason is that the verbs in sentences (10)-(12) are active (dynamic) verbs, while those in (13)-(15) are stative verbs. It is therefore obvious that the –LV prepositional suffix cannot co-occur with stative verbs in normal situations. The above sentences can, however, be heard when extraordinary and/or unusual feelings are expressed. For instance, when one utters any of the sentences (10)-(12), two closely related interpretations can be given. The first possible interpretation is that the action expressed by the verb (be it cooking, going, or sweeping) was done on one's behalf; that is to say that one was to have done the cooking, the going, or the sweeping, but when one could not do it for one reason or the other, another individual did it on one's behalf. The second interpretation is that the action expressed by the verb favoured one. In other words, one benefitted from the action. For examples (13)-(15), the interpretation may be that the subject is abnormally or extraordinarily fat, beautiful, or tall, as the case may be. It simply means that with stative verbs, the interpretation is different; instead of benefactive as for active verbs, it is rather ambiguous.

3.1.2 Inflectional Affixes in the Indicative Negative Constructions

Negative constructions are sentence types which can be used to express rejection, denial, or a contradiction of some claims by the insertion of a negative marker to the verb root. In the Ọnịcha dialect of Igbo, the general negative marker is the suffix =rọ, while in the Central Igbo dialect, it is =ghị/=ghi. The negative suffix =rọ in Ọnịcha is invariable. In negative constructions in Igbo, the vowel prefix plays a role in inflection marking. For instance, when the subject of a negative construction is a noun (singular or plural) or plural pronoun, the verb takes a prefix, but when the subject of the negative construction is a singular pronoun, the verb does not take a prefix, as can be seen in the following examples:

16	Nnénnà	é'sírọ́	ńní
	Nnenna	pref-*vb*-neg	food
		cook-suff	
	Nnenna did not cook		
17	Ézè	á'kwụ́rọ́	ụ́'gwọ́
	Eze	pref-*vb*-neg	payment
		pay-suff	
	Eze did not pay		
18	Ùnù	ámụ̀rọ̀	ákwụ́kwọ́
	You(pl.)	pref-*vb*-neg	book
		study-suff	
	You did not study		
19	Ànyì	ákọ̀rọ̀	ụ́'gbó
	We	pref-*vb*-neg	farm
		plant-suff	
	We did not plant/We did not cultivate the farm		

20	Ò	'kwúrọ̀	ókwú
	He/she	vb-neg	speech
		speak-suff	
	He/she did not speak		
21	Ọ̀	zárọ̀	únọ̀
	He/she	vb-neg	house
		sweep-suff	
	He/she did not sweep the house.		

Table 3-V Indicative suffixes in the negative constructions

From the above data, we observe that sentences (16)-(19) contain noun subjects and plural pronouns, and they have prefixes. Sentences (20) and (21) contain singular pronouns as subjects, and they do not have prefixes. The tone of the negative suffix is conditioned by the tone of the verb root. For instance, the behaviour of the vowel suffix in (21) is conditioned by the tonal modification of the verb root. The verb root has an inherent low tone verb root.

3.2 Inflectional Affixes in Imperative Constructions

Imperative is a term used in the grammatical classification of sentence types. Imperative constructions are typically used in the expression of commands. They are characterized by the presence of the harmonizing open vowel suffix. Imperative can be affirmative or negative.

3.2.1 The Imperative Affirmative

The imperative affirmative in the Ọnịcha dialect of Igbo is formed by the affixation of the harmonizing open vowel suffix to the verb root. The following are some examples with expanded verb roots:

	VERB ROOT	IMPERATIVE	GLOSS
22	lí *eat*	lìé *eat*	Eat
23	kwú *speak*	kwùó/kwùé *speak*	Speak
24	gwù *swim*	gwùó/gwùé *swim*	Swim
25	lò *think*	lòó *think*	Think

Table 3-VI Imperative affirmatives with expanded vowels (high and low tones)

The table of vowel distribution for the imperative formed with expanded vowels in Ọnịcha can be summarized as follows:

Vowel of the Verb Root	Open Vowel Suffix (OVS)
I	E
U	o or e
O	O

Table 3-VII The Ọnịcha table of vowel distribution for the imperative formed with expanded vowels.

Affixation and Auxiliaries in Igbo

	VERB ROOT	IMPERATIVE	GLOSS
26	lí *climb*	lìá *climb*	Climb
27	sú *wash*	sùá/sùọ́ *wash*	Wash
28	mù *learn*	mùá/mùọ́ *learn*	Learn
29	zá *respond*	zàá *respond*	Respond
30	zà *sweep*	zàá *sweep*	Sweep
31	mé *do*	mèé *do*	Do
32	bẹ̀ *cut*	bẹ̀ẹ́ *cut*	Cut
33	kọ́ *narrate*	kọ̀ọ́ *narrate*	Narrate
34	kọ̀ *cultivate*	kọ̀ọ́ *cultivate*	Cultivate

Table 3-VIII Imperative affirmative with non-expanded Vowels (high and low tones)

The table of vowel distribution for the imperative formed with non-expanded vowels in Ọnịcha Igbo can be summarized as follows:

Vowel of the Verb Root	Open Vowel Suffix (OVS)
ị	A
ụ	a or ọ
A	A
ẹ	ẹ
ọ	ọ

Table 3-IX The Onicha table of vowel distribution for the imperative formed with non-expanded vowels.

The above are the singular expressions of the imperative affirmative. The imperative affirmative can also be expressed in the plural form. This is done by suffixing the plural marker *–nù* to the singular imperative form, as in the following:

	VERB ROOT	IMPERATIVE SINGULAR	IMPERATIVE PLURAL
35	lí *eat*	lìé *eat*	lìénù *eat* pl.
36	sú *pound*	sùé/sùó *pound*	sùènù/sùónù *pound* pl.
37	gwù *swim*	gwùé/gwùó *swim*	gwùénù/gwùónù *swim* pl.
38	zà *sweep*	zàá *sweep*	zàánù *sweep* pl.
39	lò *think*	lòó *think*	lòónù *think* pl.
40	mẹ́ *do*	mẹ̀ẹ́ *do*	mẹ̀ẹ́nù *do* pl.

Table 3-X The formation of the imperative affirmative plural

From the foregoing data of imperative affirmative (both singular and plural), we observe that the tone of the verb root (high and low) are neutralized to low tone. The open vowel suffix harmonizes with the vowel of the verb root. For the plural affirmative imperative, the plural marker *-nụ/-nu* harmonizes with the vowel of the verb root, but the tone of the verb root is consistently low in all of them.

3.2.2 The Imperative Negative

The imperative negative is prohibitive in the Ọnịcha dialect of Igbo. It is formed by both processes of prefixation and suffixation. The high tone prefix e=/ẹ=/a= is affixed to the verb root which is immediately followed by the negative suffix =na. With low tone verb roots, the suffix is =nà with or without NP complement, but with high tone verb roots, the suffix is =ná only with an NP complement as we shall see later in the examples below. The expanded vowel [e] harmonizes with the expanded vowel verb roots and is therefore prefixed to them while the non-expanded vowels ẹ=/a= harmonize with the non-expanded vowel verb roots and are prefixed to them. The prefix ẹ= co-occurs only with the verb root containing the vowel [ẹ], while the prefix a= co-occurs with the rest of the non-expanded vowels. The negative suffix =na occurs with both expanded and non-expanded vowels. Below are some examples:

	VERB ROOT	IMPERATIVE NEGATIVE WITH NP COMPLEMENT
41	lí *eat*	é'líná ńní *don't eat food*
42	gó *buy*	é'góná àgwà *don't buy beans*
43	mẹ́ *do*	ẹ́'mẹ́ná 'njọ́ *don't do evil*
44	lí *climb*	á'líná é'nú *don't climb up*
45	Gwù *swim*	égwùnà ḿmí'lí *don't swim*
46	zà *sweep*	ázànà únò *don't sweep the house*
47	dì *endure*	édìnà ágụ́'ụ́ *don't endure hunger*
48	wẹ̀ *take*	ẹ́wẹ̀nà é'gó *don't take money*

Table 3-XI Imperative negative construction in Ọnịcha with both expanded and non-expanded vowel verb roots (high and low tone) with NP complements of the verbs.

We observe from the foregoing examples that the high tone verbs maintain their inherent high tones before the NP complement and the low tone verbs also maintain their inherent low tones before the NP complements. The different prefixes harmonize with the vowel of their respective verb roots.

	VERB ROOT	IMPERATIVE NEGATIVE WITHOUT NP COMPLEMENT
49	lí *eat*	é'línâ *don't eat*
50	gó *buy*	é'gónâ *don't buy*
51	mẹ́ *do*	ẹ́'mẹ́nâ *don't do*
52	lí *climb*	á'línâ *don't climb*
53	gwù *swim*	égwùnà *don't swim*
54	zà *sweep*	ázànà *don't sweep*
55	dì *endure*	édìnà *don't endure*
56	wẹ̀ *take*	ẹ́wẹ̀nà *don't take*
57	zù *train/breed*	ázùnà *don't train/breed*

Table 3-XII Imperative negative constructions in Ọnịcha with both expanded and non-expanded vowel verb roots (high and low) without NP complements of the verbs.

From the above data, we observe the tonal modification in the imperative suffix =na. While the low tone verb roots maintain their inherent low tones in (53-57), the high tone verb roots do not maintain their lexical tones. (49-52) witness a grammatical falling tone in the imperative suffix =nâ. The explanation of this behaviour in tone may be due to the absence of the NP complement. It is the compensatory morpheme that replaces the NP complement.

3.3 Inflectional Affixes in Imperfective Constructions

Imperfective is, according to Comrie (1976:24) an explicit reference to the internal temporal structure of a situation, viewing a situation from within. We shall, for clarity, group under the imperfective construction all the verb forms that express unfulfilled action in the present, including the future forms. In other words, all actions that are still going on at the moment of speaking – the *na* and the *kọ* forms (in Ọnịcha) will be discussed under the imperfective as well; the habitual present forms will also be subsumed under the imperfective construction, because they have the same form or structure with the present progressive. We shall therefore examine the following under the present continuous form.

3.3.1 The Present Continuous Form
- the present progressive affirmative   -   the *na* form
- the present progressive negative   -   the *dị* form
- the present imminent affirmative   -   the *kọ* form
- the present imminent negative   -   the *kọrọ* form

3.3.1.1 The Present Progressive Form
3.3.1.1a The Present Progressive Affirmative

The Ọnịcha Igbo present progressive affirmative expresses an affirmative action which goes on at the moment of speaking. The action expressed by the present progressive is unfulfilled in the sense that the speaker does not witness the completion of the action since it is still in progress at the time of speaking. The same form is used in expressing habitual actions. The present progressive affirmative in Ọnịcha dialect of Igbo is formed by the progressive marker –'na' followed by the verb to which the participial prefix is affixed, as in the following examples:

58	Ngózí nà-*à*kwá ákwà Ngozi prog-*pref*-vb cloth Ngozi is sewing cloth/Ngozi sews cloths/Ngozi is a tailor	[sew]
59	Chûkà nà-*à*gụ́ ákwụ́kwọ́ Chuka prog-*pref*-vb book Chuka is reading a book/Chuka reads/Chuka is a student	[read]
60	Fá nà-*á*zà ụ́nọ̀ They prog-*pref*-vb house They are sweeping the house/They are sweepers/They are cleaners	[sweep]

61	Ànyí nà-*ákọ̀* ú'gbó We prog-*pref*-vb farm We are cultivating the farm/We are farmers	[cultivate]
62	Ọ́ nà-*èdẹ̀* ákwúkwọ́ He/she prog-*pref*-vb book He/she is writing a book/He/she is a writer/He/she is a secretary	[write]

Table 3-XIII The present progressive affirmative

From the foregoing examples, we observe that the progressive marker *na* always precedes a prefix which is affixed to the verb root. The tone of the progressive marker is consistently low, while that of the prefix is determined by the tone of the verb root. For instance, there is tonal polarization; in other words, the prefix takes a low tone if the verb root has a high tone, and a high tone if the verb root has a low tone.

From the point of view of interpretation of the above sentences, we observe that apart from expressing the fact that the action is going on right now at the moment of speaking; it also indicates that the action goes on habitually. In other words, it means that each of the sentences is a regular event which occurs consistently. The context determines whether the action is momentary or habitual. Kelly (1954:14) calls the habitual present form in Ọnịcha Igbo the present indefinite. We can therefore say that the present progressive in Ọnịcha expresses durative, iterative aspects.

3.3.1.1b The Present Progressive Negative

The present progressive negative form in the Ọnịcha dialect is formed by the presence of the negative progressive marker 'dị' to which is suffixed the general negative marker =rọ, followed by the verb to which is prefixed the harmonizing participial vowel prefix as in the following examples:

63	Úchè á'*dírọ́* àkwá ákwà Uche pref-neg prog pref-vb cloth 　　　marker　　　sew Uche does not sew cloth/Uche is not a tailor
64	Chûka á'*dírọ́* àgụ́ ákwúkwọ́ Chuka pref-neg prog pref-vb book 　　　marker　　　read Chuka is not reading/Chuka does not read/Chuka is not a student
65	Fà á'*dírọ́* àzà ụ́nọ̀ They pref-neg prog pref-vb house 　　　marker　　　sweep They are not sweeping the house/They don't sweep the house/They are not sweepers
66	Ànyí á'*dírọ́* àkọ̀ ú'gbó We pref-neg prog pref-vb farm 　　　marker　　　cultivate We are not farming/We don't farm/We are not farmers

67	Ọ̀	dị́rọ́	èdẹ̀	ákwụ́kwọ́
	He/she	neg prog marker	pref-*vb* *write*	book
	He/she is not writing He/she does not write/He/she is not a writer			

Table 3-XIV The present progressive negative

The above examples are deep structure realizations. In actual utterance or the surface structure realizations, the general negative suffix =*rọ* is deleted so that the above examples will be realized without =*rọ*, as in the following:

68. Úchè á'dị̀ àkwá ákwà
69. Ọ̀ dị́ èdẹ̀ ákwụ́kwọ́

From the data above, we observe the following:

a. the presence of the progressive negative marker. The prefix 'a' is attached to the negative marker only when the subject is a noun or a plural pronoun and the harmonizing verbal vowel prefix is affixed to the verb root. There is a consistent presence of downstep on the negative marker with subject nouns and plural pronoun subjects, as seen in the examples (63-66).

b. the progressive negative marker is self-sufficient in expressing negation in Igbo, that is, the negative suffix marker is deleted in the synchronic usage.

From the point of view of meaning, the present progressive negative expresses an action which can be interpreted in three ways:

a. It expresses that the action is not going on now.
b. It expresses that the action does not normally go on.
c. It describes the agent as non-professional of the action expressed by the verb.

Note that the present progressive affirmative describes the agent as the professional of the action expressed by the verb.

3.3.1.2 The Present Imminent Form
3.3.1.2a The Present Imminent Affirmative
The present imminent affirmative in Ọnịcha expresses an action which is going on at the moment of speaking. It can also express an action which will take place immediately after the moment of speaking. The present imminent affirmative marker =*kọ* has a fixed collocation with the verb root jẹ *go*. It is formed by suffixing the present imminent marker =*kọ* to the verb root, as in the following examples:

70	Àdá	jèkọ̀		í'sí	ńní
	Ada	vb-*Pr.immi*		pref-*vb*	food
		marker		*cook*	
	Ada is going to cook				
71	Ńnẹ́	yá	jèkọ̀	áfịá	
	Mother	his/her	vb-*Pr.immi*	market	
			go-*marker*		
	His/her mother is going to the market				

Table 3-XV The present imminent affirmative

With reference to the above sentences, we observe that sentence (70) can be interpreted either as prospective present because of the presence of the infinitive í'sí *to cook* following the verb or as an obligation. In the prospective context, Ada is seen as preparing for the process of cooking food. It can, in another context, be seen as an obligation that 'Ada should cook food'. In sentence (71), the present imminent construction functions like indicative affirmative. If the child is asked:

73	Ńnẹ́	'yá	ọ̀	jèkọ̀	èbẹ́'ẹ́
	Mother	his/her	pro	vb-*Pr.immi*	where
				go-*marker*	
	Where is his/her mother going?				

The response should be:

74	Ńnẹ́	'yá	jèkọ̀	áfịá	
	Mother	his/her	vb-*Pr.immi*	market	
			go-*marker*		
	His/her mother is going to market				

Table 3-XVI The present imminent affirmative (continued)

to mean that the mother is either preparing to go to market or is already on her way to the market. We also observe that if the present imminent marker is followed by a verb, the verb must be in the infinitive form, as in sentence (70). It can also be followed by a noun as in sentence (71). The tone of the present imminent marker is low and it affects the tone of the verb root with the result that it looks structurally like an indicative construction where the verbal elements are neutralized to low tones.

3.3.1.2b The Present Imminent Negative

The present imminent negative in Ọnịcha expresses an action which does not take place at the moment of speaking or an action which does not habitually take place. The following are some examples:

Affixation and Auxiliaries in Igbo

75	Àdá	é'jékọ́rọ́		í'sí	ńní
	Ada	pref-*vb*-Pr.immi.<u>neg</u>	pref-*vb*		food
		go-marker	cook		
	Ada is not going to cook				
76	Ńnẹ	'yá	é'jékọ́rọ́		áfíá
	Mother	his/her	pref-*vb*-Pr.immi.<u>neg</u>		market
			go-marker		
	His/her mother is not going to the market				
77	Ọ̀	jé'kọ́rọ́	í'kwú	úgwọ́	áfù
	He/she	vb-*Pr.immi.*<u>neg</u>	pref-*vb*	payment	that
		go-*marker*	pay		
	He/she is not going to pay that debt				

Table 3-XVII *The present imminent negative*

From the foregoing examples, we observe the following:

a. that the present imminent negative is formed by suffixing the present imminent marker =*kọ* to which is also suffixed the negative suffix =*rọ* to the verb root.
b. that the present imminent marker and the negative marker both take a downstep in all the constructions.
c. the insertion of verbal vowel prefix with subject nouns and its deletion with singular pronoun subject, as in (75), (76) and (77).
d. that the present imminent negative expression is more of rejection than simple negative indication. For instance, sentences (75-77) can more naturally be glossed as:

78. Ada will not cook
79. His/her mother will not go to the market
80. He/she will not pay that debt

3.3.2 The Expression of the Future Form
Gá, in Ọnịcha is a general future marker and, from the examples realized from this verb, it is observed that, apart from expressing a future time event, *ga* expresses some other modal meanings, including:

- Willingness
- Intention
- Prediction
- Compulsion/Obligation

3.3.2a The Future Affirmative Form
The future affirmative form in the Ọnịcha dialect of Igbo is formed by the future marker –*ga* followed by the verb to which a harmonizing verbal vowel prefix is affixed, as in the following examples:

81	Ézè	gà	èchí	ọ́'zọ́	
	Eze	aux.fut. marker	pref-*vb* *crown*	title	
	Eze will take (on) a title				
82	Ànyị́	gà	àgbá	é'gwú	
	We	aux.fut. marker	pref-*vb* *dance*	dance	
	We will dance				
83	Fá	gà	ázà	ụ́nọ̀	
	They	aux.fut. marker	pref-*vb* *sweep*	house	
	They will sweep the house				
84	Ọ́	gà	ázụ̀	ụ́mù	'yá
	He/she	aux.fut. marker	pref-*vb* *train*	children	his/her
	He/she will train his/her children				
85	Ọ́	gà	ẹ́gẹ̀	ńtì	
	He/she	aux.fut. marker	pref-*vb* *listen*	ear	
	He/she will listen				

Table 3-XVIII The future affirmative form

From the foregoing data, we observe that the tone on the future marker *ga* is consistently low, just as in the present progressive affirmative. The tone of the prefix is determined by that of the verb root. For instance, if the verb root has a low tone, the verbal prefix will be a high tone, as in (83), (84), (85) and if the verb root has high tone, the verbal prefix will be low toned, as in (81) and (82). The future form in Ọnịcha is grouped as imperfective because the action expressed by the verb is not fulfilled and may, in some cases, never be fulfilled. The intention/wish of the speaker may or may not be realized.

3.3.2b The Future Negative Form

The future negative in Ọnịcha Igbo is an expression of rejection, inhibition, denial, or contradiction. It expresses what will not happen or what will not be done. It is formed by the future negative marker –*ma* followed by the verb to which a harmonizing verbal vowel prefix is affixed, as in the following examples:

86	Chûkà	á'<u>má</u>	áñụ́	ḿ'mányá
	Chuka	pref-<u>fut.neg</u>	pref-*vb* marker *drink*	wine
	Chuka will not drink wine			
87	Ànyị́	á'<u>ma</u>	ázụ́	á'fị́á
	We	pref-<u>fut.neg</u>	pref-*vb* marker *trade*	market
	We will not trade			

Affixation and Auxiliaries in Igbo 51

88	Fà	á'<u>má</u>		á'kọ́	'jí
	They	pref-<u>fut.neg</u> marker	pref-*vb*	*cultivate*	yam
	They will not cultivate yam					
89	Ọ̀	má		'ázà	únọ̀
	He/she	fut.neg. marker	pref-*vb*	*sweep*	house
	He/she will not sweep the house					
90	Ọ̀	má		'égwú	é'gwú
	He/she	fut.neg. marker	pref-*vb*	*play*	play
	He/she will not play					

Table 3-XIX The future negative form

From the data above, we observe that the future negative marker *ma* takes a vowel prefix when constructed with a noun subject or a plural pronoun subject. The tone on the vowel prefix is high, while that on the future negative marker is downstep high (i.e. if preceded by a vowel prefix). With high tone verb roots, the tone on the participial prefix is high, as in (86) and (87), but with low tone verb roots, the tone of the verb root is raised to a downstep, as in (88) (i.e. if the subject is a noun or plural pronoun). If the subject is a singular pronoun, the future negative marker will not take a prefix, and if the following verb is low toned, the participial prefix takes a downstep tone.

3.4 Inflectional Affixes in Perfective Constructions

The term, *perfective* has been variously called the *Perfect Tense*, (Swift et al., 1962); *Subject Verb Form II, Main*, (Green and Igwe, 1963); *Completive*, (Welmers and Welmers); *La- form of the Verb*, (Ward 1936) (Source: Emenanjo 1978:179). Comrie (1976:18) defines *perfective* as a term used in indicating a completed action. In perfective constructions, the action expressed by the verb is viewed as a whole irrespective of the time contrast which may be part of it. Perfective (fulfilled) can contrast with Imperfective (unfulfilled) which we have discussed above. Under the perfective constructions in Ọnịcha, we shall consider the following:

- the future perfective affirmative
- the future perfective negative
- the present perfective affirmative
- the present perfective negative
- the past perfective
- the unfulfilled perfective affirmative
- the unfulfilled perfective negative

3.4.1 The Future Perfective
3.4.1a The Future Perfective Affirmative

The future perfective affirmative in Ọnịcha is expressed via a combination of the affirmative auxiliary *ga* followed by the participial prefix affixed to the verb to which is suffixed the perfective suffix =*go* is added. The following are examples of the affirmative perfective constructions in Ọnịcha Igbo:

91	Àmáká	gà	èsígó	'jí
	Amaka	aux.	pref-*vb*-perf.suff. *cook*	yam
	Amaka will/must have cooked yam			
92	Fá	gà	àwụ́gó	'árụ́
	They	aux.	pref-*vb*-perf.suff. *wash*	body
	They will/must have taken their bath			
93	Àdá	gà	ázàgó	ụ́nọ̀
	Ada	aux.	pref-*vb*-perf.suff. *sweep*	house
	Ada will/must have swept the house			
94	Òbí	gà	ékwúgó	ó'kwú
	Obi	aux.	pref-*vb*-perf.suff. *speak*	speech
	Obi will/must have spoken			
95	Ọ́	gà	èmẹ́gó	ǹjọ́
	He/she	aux.	pref-*vb*-perf.suff. *do*	evil
	He/she will/must have committed sin			

Table 3-XX The future perfective affirmative

From the data above, we observe that the affirmative auxiliary *ga*, which functioned as a simple future auxiliary in the future construction above, now functions as a modalizer because of the presence of the perfective suffix =*go*. If the suffix =*go* is deleted in all the constructions above, each of the sentences will be interpreted as a simple future form. The perfective suffix has only one form in the Ọnịcha dialect of Igbo, i.e. it has only one form which co-occurs with both expanded and non-expanded vowels. The auxiliary *ga* maintains a low tone in all the constructions in which it appears. In the Ọnịcha dialect, we observe that the perfective suffix is affixed to the participle, while in the Central Igbo dialect, it is affixed to the auxiliary. The tone of the perfective suffix is invariable in Ọnịcha Igbo; it is consistently high toned in all the data above. When the object following a perfective suffix has a low-high tone, the low tone is raised to a step tone. When the object is a monosyllabic noun, the high tone of the monosyllabic noun is reduced to a step tone, as in (91). If the perfective suffix precedes a high-high tone object, the second high tone is reduced to a step tone,

Affixation and Auxiliaries in Igbo 53

as in (94); and when the perfective suffix precedes a high-low tone object, the tones remain unchanged, as in (93). The future perfective expresses probability.

3.4.1b The Future Perfective Negative
The future perfective negative in Ọnịcha Igbo is formed by the combination of the negative auxiliary 'ma' followed by the participial prefix attached to the verb to which the perfective suffix '=go' is added. The following are some examples:

96	Fà	á'má	égógó	'jí
	They	pref-<u>neg</u>	pref-*vb*-perf.suff.	yam
		aux	*buy*	
	They will/must not have bought yam			
97	Íké	á'má	ásụ́gó	á'kwụ́
	Ike	pref-<u>neg</u>	pref-*vb*-perf.suff.	palmnut
		aux	*pound*	
	Ike will/must not have pounded (the) palmnuts			
98	Ọ̀	má	'álụ́gó	ọ́'lụ́
	He/she	neg.aux.	pref-*vb*-perf.suff.	work
			work	
	He/she will/must not have worked			
99	Ọ̀	má	'ázàgó	únọ̀
	He/she	neg.aux.	pref-*vb*-perf.suff.	house
			sweep	
	He/she will/must not have swept the house			

Table 3-XXI The future perfective negative

From the above data, we observe the presence of a negative auxiliary which has a consistently high tone. With a noun or a plural pronoun subject, the negative auxiliary carries a step tone because of the vowel prefix (which carries a high tone) affixed to it. The participial prefixes remain high with high tone verb roots, as in (96-98), but with low tone verb roots, the participial prefix is a step tone, as in (99). The tone of the perfective suffix is invariable – always high.

When the auxiliary, whether in affirmative or negative construction, combines with the perfective suffix, the output is quite different from the interpretations we had without the perfective suffix. What results from the combination is a hypothetical statement. For instance, each of the examples above assumes that the action expressed by the verb must not have been accomplished before the report. It also expresses probability.

3.4.2 The Present Perfective
3.4.2a The Present Perfective Affirmative
The present perfective affirmative form in Ọnịcha dialect is formed by suffixing the perfective suffix =*go* to the verb root to which is also prefixed the participial prefix. In the French language, the construction is known as *passé composé*, (which is

aspectual) while in English, it is called the *present perfect verb form*. The present perfective verb form expresses a completed action whose effect is still felt in the present. The following are some examples of the present perfective affirmative construction in Ọnịcha Igbo:

100   Íbè   àl*ú*gó   ọ́'lụ́
       Ibe   pref-*vb*-perf.suff.   *work*   work
       Ibe has done the work/Ibe has worked

101   Únù   è*ch*úgó   ḿ'mílí
       You(pl.)   pref-*vb*-perf.suff.   *fetch*   water
       You have fetched water

102   Fá   è*d*ẹ́gó   ákwà
       They   pref-*vb*-perf.suff.   *iron*   cloth
       They have ironed the clothing

103   Ànyị   á*z*àgó   'íló
       We   pref-*vb*-perf.suff.   *sweep* compound
       We have swept the compound

104   Ó   *gw*ùgó   é'gwú
       He/she   *vb*-perf.suff. *play*   play
       He/she has played

Table 3-XXII The present perfective verb form

From the above data, we observe that the present perfective construction is a direct contrast of the present progressive construction which is an imperfective construction. We observe that the present perfective affirmative does not require any auxiliary verb. The perfective suffix affixed to the verb root expresses the action that is completed, but its effect is relevant in the present time. The tonal behaviour of this verb form resembles that of the future perfective negative. The tone of the participial prefix is conditioned by the tone of the verb root.

3.4.2b The Present Perfective Negative
The present perfective negative in Ọnịcha Igbo is realized in the same way as the unfulfilled perfective negative, and so will be examined along with it in a succeeding section.

3.4.3 The Past Perfective
The past perfective affirmative form, like its present perfective counterpart in Ọnịcha Igbo, is formed by a combination of the perfective suffix =*go* and the extensional suffix =*lị* which are affixed to the verb root, to which is also affixed the participial prefix when and only when the subject of the construction is either a noun or a plural pronoun. The past perfective form expresses a past action which is remote at the time

of speaking. It is also aspectual. The following are some examples of past perfective affirmative constructions in the Ọnịcha dialect of Igbo.

105	Àdá èchúgólì m'mílí Ada pref-*vb*-perf-<u>ext</u> water *fetch*-suff-<u>suff</u> Ada had already fetched water
106	Ǹnà yá àkwúgólì úgwọ́ ákwúkwọ́ Father his/her pref-*vb*-perf-<u>ext</u> payment book *pay*-suff-<u>suff</u> His/her father had already paid school fees
107	Òbí èjégólì á'fịá Obi pref-*vb*-perf-<u>ext</u> market *go*-suff-<u>suff</u> Obi had already gone to market
108	Ó gógólì ákwúkwọ́ He/she vb-*perf*-<u>ext</u> book buy-*suff*-<u>suff</u> He/she had already bought books
109	Ó zàgólì únọ̀ He/she vb-*perf*-<u>ext</u> house sweep-*suff*-<u>suff</u> He/she had already swept the house

Table 3-XXIII The past perfective form

From the foregoing data, we observe that the past perfective, like the present perfective discussed above, does not take an auxiliary verb. The perfective suffix =*go* has a consistent high tone, while the extensional suffix =*li* has a low tone in all the constructions above. We observe also that it is the extensional suffix =*li* which marks the anteriority in the past perfective constructions above and gives the sentences the past perfective nature, otherwise, it can be present perfective affirmative.

3.4.4 The Unfulfilled Perfective
3.4.4a The Unfulfilled Perfective Affirmative

The unfulfilled perfective affirmative construction in Ọnịcha dialect of Igbo is a construction where the desire or hope expressed by the verb has not been realized even though it is supposed to have been accomplished before the moment of speaking. It is formed by a combination of the unfulfilled marker –*ka* (henceforth, um), the verb root, and the perfective suffix. When the unfulfilled marker is followed by the verb root to which the participial prefix *a=/e=/ẹ=* and the perfective suffix =*go* are affixed, an unfulfilled perfective construction results. The following are some of the examples of such constructions in Ọnịcha Igbo.

110	Àdá	'á<u>ká</u>	'élígó	ńní
	Ada	pref-<u>um</u>	pref-*vb*-perf.suff.	food
			eat	
	Ada should have eaten food			
111	Fá	'á<u>ká</u>	'ákwụ́gó	ụ́'gwọ́
	They	pref-<u>um</u>	pref-*vb*-perf.suff.	payment
			pay	
	They should have paid the debt			
112	Ànyí	'á<u>ká</u>	àzàgò	únọ̀
	We	pref-<u>um</u>	pref-*vb*-perf.suff.	house
			sweep	
	We should have swept the house			
113	Ọ́	'<u>ká</u>	'ẹ́dẹ́gó	ákwụ́kwọ́
	He/she	<u>um</u>	pref-*vb*-perf.suff.	book
			write	
	He/she should have written a book/He should have written a letter			
114	Í	'<u>ká</u>	àmụ̀gò	ọ́lụ́
	You(sing)	<u>um</u>	pref-*vb*-perf.suff.	work
			learn	
	You should have learnt a trade			

Table 3-XXIV The unfulfilled perfective affirmative

From the above data, we observe that the unfulfilled marker maintains a step tone in all the constructions. The high tone verbs maintain their inherent tones, while the low tone verbs maintain their inherent low tones, as in the examples above. The perfective suffix =*go* copies the tone of the verb root, as in examples (112) and (114). We observe also that the unfulfilled marker (i.e. auxiliary) produces a modalizing effect when combined with a perfective suffix in a construction. For instance, the examples above are all hypothetical sentences because the actions are supposed to have been completed before the time of speaking. The unfulfilled marker has only one form; it co-occurs with both expanded and non-expanded vowels of the verb root.

3.4.4b The Unfulfilled Perfective Negative

The unfulfilled perfective negative in Ọnịcha Igbo is formed when the unfulfilled marker –*ka* is followed by the verb root to which are affixed the participial prefix *a=/e=/ẹ=* and the negative suffix =*rọ*. In the Central Igbo dialect, this construction is formed by the affixation of the perfective negative suffix =*beghi* to the verb root. The following are some of the examples of the unfulfilled perfective negative constructions in Ọnịcha Igbo:

115	Íbè	á'<u>ká</u>	èlíró	ń'ní
	Ibe	pref-<u>um</u>	pref-*vb*-neg.suff.	food
			eat	
	Ibe has not eaten (food) yet			

Affixation and Auxiliaries in Igbo

116	Fà	á'ká	àkwụ́rọ́	ụ́'gwọ́
	They	pref-<u>um</u>	pref-*vb*-neg.suff.	payment
			pay	
	They have not paid yet/They have not yet paid			
117	Ùnù	á'ká	àmụ́rọ́	ákwụ́kwọ́
	You(pl)	pref-<u>um</u>	pref-*vb*-neg.suff.	book
			learn	
	You have not studied yet			
118	Ọ̀	ká	àzàrọ́	ụ́nọ̀
	He/she	<u>um</u>	pref-*vb*-neg.suff.	house
			sweep	
	He/she has not yet swept the house			
119	Ì	ká	ègwùrọ́	é'gwú
	You (sing.) <u>um</u>		pref-*vb*-neg.suff.	play
			play	
	You have not yet played			

Table 3-XXV The unfulfilled perfective negative

From the above examples, we observe the tonal morphology of the unfulfilled marker; in the unfulfilled perfective affirmative, the step tone affects both the unfulfilled marker and its prefix; the participial prefix attached to high tone verbs has step tone, while the participial prefix attached to low tone verbs has low tone. In the unfulfilled perfective negative, the unfulfilled marker has step tone with subject nouns and plural pronouns; with singular pronouns, however, it has a high tone. The participial prefix in all the constructions has low tone. As earlier noted, the present perfective negative and the unfulfilled perfective negative are expressed in exactly the same way in the Ọnịcha dialect. Both are expressed just as in the examples we have presented in the unfulfilled perfective negative (nos [115-119] above).

We observe that in verbal constructions, certain verb forms use inflectional suffixes, auxiliaries, verbal vowel prefixes, and syntactic tone pattern to mark different inflections. It is pertinent to state that whereas some constructions take auxiliaries, others do not. For instance, the indicative and the imperative constructions do not need prefix in their inflections except in their negative constructions. The perfective and imperfective constructions need the auxiliary verb in all their constructions with the exception of the present imminent (affirmative and negative) and the present and past perfective affirmative.

3.5 Recapitulatory Table of Inflectional Verbal Affixes in Ọnịcha Igbo

			Aux	Prefix	Suffix
1		**Indicative Constructions**			
	I	Indicative Affirmative	-	-	=LV
	Ii	Indicative Negative	-	a=/e=/ẹ= with subject nouns and plural pronouns – with singular pronouns	=rọ
2		**Imperative Constructions**			
	I	Imperative Affirmative	-	-	=e/=o (with expanded vowels); =a/=ẹ/=ọ (with non-expanded vowels)
	Ii	Imperative Negative	-	e=/ẹ=/a=	=nâ (with high tone vowels); =nà (low tone vowels)
3		**Imperfective Constructions**			
	I	Present Progressive Affirmative	Na	a=/e=/ẹ=	-
	Ii	Present Progressive Negative	Di	a=/e=/ẹ=	-
	Iii	Present Imminent Affirmative	-	-	=kọ̀
	Iv	Present Imminent Negative	-	ẹ=	=kọ́rọ́
	V	Future Affirmative	Ga	a=/e=/ẹ=	-
	Vi	Future Negative	Ma	a=/e=/ẹ=	-
4		**Perfective Constructions**			
	I	Future Perfective Affirmative	Gà	a=/e=/ẹ=	=go
	Ii	Future Perfective Negative	Má	a=/e=/ẹ=	=go
	Iii	Present Perfective Affirmative	-	a=/e=/ẹ=	=go
	Iv	Present Perfective Negative	Ka	a=/e=/ẹ=	=rọ
	V	Past Perfective	-	a=/e=/ẹ=	=goli

				Aux	Prefix	Suffix
5		**Unfulfilled Constructions**	**Perfective**			
	I	Unfulfilled Affirmative	Perfective	Ka	a=/e=/ẹ=	**=go**
	Ii	**Unfulfilled Negative**	**Perfective**	**Ka**	**a=/e=/ẹ=**	**=rọ**

Table 3-XXVI Inflectional verbal affixes in Ọnịcha

Chapter 4

Morpho-Syntactic Features of Derivational Affixes

Introduction
This chapter discusses the morpho-syntactic analysis of derivational affixes in the Ọnịcha dialect of Igbo. It examines the derivational processes according to the position of the affixes in the word as in the following sub-headings: The chapter concludes with a summary of the derivative affixes in the Ọnịcha Igbo lect.

4.1   Prefixation
Prefixation in Ọnịcha Igbo involves the derivations of the infinitive and the participle, the processes of derivation involving prefixation and reduplication (whether total or partial) and prefixation and suffixation are also considered under prefixation.

4.2   Interfixation
Interfixation involves the derivation of words in which the affix occurs between two identical or sometimes non identical roots. It is a situation where the affix interrupts the sequence of two roots. Interfixation as a process of derivation is grouped according to the nature of the base, hence there are noun-base form and verb-base form of interfixation in the Ọnịcha Igbo lect.

4.3   Circumfixation
Circumfixation involves the derivation of words in the dialect where both prefix and suffix are simultaneously employed to express one semantic meaning. In circumfixation, there is a paradigm or what may be termed a circumfixal frame where the base form or the verb root is inserted to derive the new word.

4.4   Deverbatives
This is a process of derivation which results in the formation of nouns from verbs. The derived nominals have morphological resemblance with the verb root from which they are derived. This section demonstrates the importance of tone as an affix which is used for derivation. The tone carried by a word is an essential feature of its meaning.

Derivational affixes serve to derive new words and can sometimes change the word class of the verb root to which they are attached. Igbo is a verb language, therefore, the verb serves, for the most part, as the base for deriving other words. We shall consider the derivational processes in Ọnịcha Igbo under the following headings:

    a. Prefixation
    b. Interfixation
    c. Circumfixation
    d. Deverbatives
    e. Tonalization

4.1 Prefixation

Prefixation is a morphological term which denotes the affixing of the appropriate derivational prefix to the given root. In the Ọnịcha dialect of Igbo, prefixation can bring about the derivation of the infinitive and the participle, which are treated as nomino-verbals. We shall, in what follows, discuss the derivation of the infinitive and the participle in Ọnịcha Igbo.

4.1.1 The Infinitive

The infinitive, as defined by Quirk & Greenbaum (1973:39), is a non-finite verb form that has neither tense distinctions nor modals. There is no concord/agreement between the subject and the verb in the infinitive constructions. It is a verbal derivative which, in Igbo, is formed by prefixing a high tone harmonizing close vowel í-/ị́- to the verb root. The Ọnịcha Igbo infinitive has both nominal and verbal qualities; hence, it is classed as a nomino-verbal. It is nominal when it performs certain functions of a noun; for instance, appearing in sentence positions where a noun could be substitutable. It is also verbal when it displays certain characteristics of a verb – like associating with objects and adverbial modifiers. In isolation, the Ọnịcha Igbo infinitive can be said to have a semantic representation which does not represent any definite semantic idea apart from the undetermined denotative sense. It can be likened to a virtual image. The infinitives in Igbo exist in clusters, and so, in isolation, they pose different problems, especially with respect to homonyms, where different meanings are expressed with the same phonological shape. The intended meanings of the homonyms cannot be captured unless the appropriate complement is attached. For instance, the infinitive í'gbá in isolation, cannot be assigned a definite or specific value because it can generate a lot of interpretations ranging from *running* to *prophesying*. It is only an appropriate complement that can limit the reference of the infinitive in Igbo. The following are some of the examples of the derivations of simple infinitives in Ọnịcha Igbo.

	PREFIX	HIGH TONE VERB ROOT	INIFINITIVE	GLOSS
1	í-	lí *eat*	í'lí	*to eat*
2	í-	kwú *speak*	í'kwú	*to speak/talk*
3	í-	zó *hide*	í'zó	*to hide*
4	í-	chí *crown*	í'chí	*to crown/ordain*
5	í-	gó *buy*	í'gó	*to buy*

Table 4-I Ọnịcha infinitives formed with expanded vowel prefix í= (high tone verb root)

	PREFIX	HIGH TONE VERB ROOT	INFINITIVE	GLOSS
6	ị́-	lị́ *climb*	ị́'lị́	*to climb*
7	ị́-	kwụ́ *stand*	ị́'kwụ́	*to stand, to pay*
8	ị́-	mẹ́ *do*	ị́'mẹ́	*to do*
9	ị́-	chọ́ *seek*	ị́'chọ́	*to seek*
10	ị́-	zá *respond*	ị́'zá	*to respond, to swell*

Table 4-II Ọnịcha infinitives formed with non-expanded vowel prefix ị́= (high tone verb roots).

Affixation and Auxiliaries in Igbo

	PREFIX í=	LOW TONE VERB ROOT	INFINITIVE	GLOSS
11	í-	nì *bury*	Ínì	*to bury*
12	í-	zù *meet*	Ízù	*to meet*
13	í-	lò *think*	Ílò	*to think*
14	í-	sò *follow*	Ísò	*to follow*

Table 4-III Ọnịcha infinitives formed with expanded vowel prefix.

	PREFIX ị̈=	LOW TONE VERB ROOT	INFINITIVE	GLOSS
15	ị́-	zà *sweep*	ị́zà	*to sweep*
16	ị́-	zụ̀ *train*	ị́zụ̀	*to train*
17	ị́-	nọ̀ *stay*	ị́nọ̀	*to stay*
18	ị́-	bẹ̀ *cut, end*	ị́bẹ̀	*to cut, to end*
19	ị́-	chị̀ *shout*	ị́chị̀	*to shout*

Table 4-IV Ọnịcha infinitives formed with non-expanded vowel prefix ị́= (low tone verb roots).

From the foregoing examples, we observe the following:

a. Infinitives formed with high tone verb roots in both the expanded and the non-expanded vowels have the high tone of the verb root lowered to a downstep in the derived form.
b. Infinitives formed with low tone verb roots in both the expanded and the non-expanded vowels remain low in their derived form. The simple infinitive in Ọnịcha Igbo is formed through a systematic process of prefixation of high tone vowel prefix í=/ị́= to the expanded and non-expanded verb roots depending on the ATR quality of the vowel of the root.

4.1.1a The Perfective Infinitive

Morphologically speaking, the perfective infinitive is the same as the simple infinitive to which the perfective suffix =go is affixed. The perfective infinitive is commonly formed in Ọnịcha with the modal verb -kwẹ̀sị̀ *ought to/should have*. This modal verb expresses an obligation/supposition which is a weak obligation and cannot be compared with the obligation expressed with the modal auxiliary *ga* (cf the expression of the future form above). The following are examples of constructions in Ọnịcha Igbo using the perfective infinitive derivative.

20	Fá	kwẹ̀sị̀	í'*lú*gó	únọ̀
	They	should have	pref-*vb*-perf.suff *build*	house
	They should have built a house			

21	Ànyị́	kwẹ̀sị̀	í'*lí*gó	ńní
	We	should have	pref-*vb*-perf.suff *eat*	food
	We should have eaten (food)			

22	Ọ́ kwẹ̀sị̀lị̀ ízàgò ìló
	He/she should have pref-*vb*-perf.suff compound
	sweep
	He/she should have swept the compound
23	Úchè kwẹ̀sị̀lị̀ ínọ̀gò ẹ́bẹ́ à
	Uche should have pref-*vb*-perf.suff where this
	stay
	Uche should have been here

Table 4-V The perfective infinitive constructions

From the above data, we observe that the perfective infinitive complements the modal verb *kwẹ̀sị̀lị̀*. Sometimes, a completive suffix =*si* precedes the perfective suffix attached to the verb and the two suffixes constitute a suffix =*sigo* which, when attached to the verb root, gives a completive notion of the construction, as in the following:

24	Àdá kwẹ̀sị̀lị̀ í'lúsígó ọ́lú áfù
	Ada ought to pref-*vb*-ext.suff-<u>perf.suff</u> work that
	work
	Ada ought to have finished that work
25	Ọ́ kwẹ̀sị̀lị̀ í'súsígó ákwà
	He/she ought to pref-*vb*-ext.suff-<u>perf.suff</u> cloth
	wash
	He/she ought to have finished washing clothes/the clothing
26	Únù kwẹ̀sị̀lị̀ íkọ̀sìgọ̀ ú'gbó
	You(pl.) ought to pref-*vb*-ext.suff-<u>perf.suff</u> farm
	plant
	You ought to have finished planting
27	Fá kwẹ̀sị̀lị̀ ízàsìgò únọ̀
	They ought to pref-*vb*-ext.suff-<u>perf.suff</u> house
	sweep
	They ought to have finished sweeping the house

Table 4-VI Perfective infinitive constructions with completive suffix

We observe, from the foregoing examples, that when the modal verb co-occurs with the perfective infinitive, the result is a hypothetical construction. There is the assumption that the subject has no logical reason for not fulfilling the obligation, but since the obligation expressed by the modal is weak, the consequences will not be serious if the obligation is not fulfilled. The extensional suffix =*si* has a completive effect on all the constructions. It harmonizes with the vowel of the verb root but the perfective suffix is invariable. It co-occurs with both the expanded and the non-expanded vowels. The extensional suffix =*si* and the perfective suffix =*go* copy the tone of the verb root to which they are attached.

4.1.1b Functions of Infinitive
4.1.1b.i Verbal Functions of infinitive
The infinitive cannot occur as the only verb of a simple clause. It can occur as a verbal item only if a finite verb is the first element in the verb phrase. Infinitives used with other verbs serve to modify the meaning of such other verbs, as they serve to indicate purpose, reason, or result as we can see in the following examples:

28	Ọ́ He/she He went home to cook	nà*bàlụ̀* vb-*ext.suff*-infl.suff go		í'*sí* pref-*vb* cook	ńní food
29	Ànyí We We went to see the priest	jè*lù* vb-*infl.suff* go		í'*fụ́* pref-*vb* see	ụ́kòchúkwú priest
30	Nwóké Man This man came to work	à this	bìà*lù* vb-*infl.suff* come	ị̀'*lú* pref-*vb* work	ọ́lụ́ work
31	Fá They They refused to pay	jù*lù* vb-*infl.suff* refuse		ị̀'*kwú* pref-*vb* pay	ụ́gwọ́ payment
32	Únù You(pl.) You agreed to fetch water for him	kwètàlù vb-infl.suff agree		í'*chúlú* pref-*vb*-ext.suff fetch	yá ind.obj	ḿmí'lí water

Table 4-VII Verbal functions of infinitive in Ọnịcha

From the foregoing examples, we observe that the infinitives serve as complements in the sentences. Though the constructions above are complex clauses, the presence of the infinitives helps to complete their meaning. Apart from sentence (30) which will be complete in itself without the infinitive, the rest need the infinitive for precision. For instance, in (28), (29), (30), the infinitive indicates the reason for the action of the verb. In (31), (32), the infinitive indicates the result of the action expressed by the verb.

4.1.1b.ii Infinitive as Obligatory Complement of Certain Verbs
The Ọnịcha Igbo infinitive can function as an obligatory complement of some verbs in complex sentences. Such verbs include: -chọ́ *wish*; -rápụ̀ *leave out*; nwéí'ké *can, be able*. The following are some examples:

33	Chí'ké chọ̀*lụ̀*	ị̀'*fụ́*		ńnà	'yá
	Chike	vb-*LV*	inf-*vb*	father	him
		wish-*ST*	pref-*see*		
	Chike wants to see his father				
34	Únù	rápụ̀*lụ̀*	ị̀zà	ụ́nọ̀	
	You(pl.)	vb-*LV*	inf-*vb*	house	
		leave out-*FT*	pref-*sweep*		
	You (pl.) left out sweeping the house				
35	Fá	nwẹ̀*lụ̀* íké	í'*bídó*	ọ́lụ́	
	They	vb-*LV*	power inf-*vb*	work	
		have-*ST*	pref-*start*		
	They can start the work/They have the authority to begin the work				

Table 4-VIII Infinitive as obligatory complement of certain verbs

From the above examples, we observe that the –LV suffix in examples (33) and (35) expresses present meaning because of the nature of the verbs. They are both stative verbs. It is only in example (34) that the –LV suffix expresses the past time meaning because it is a dynamic verb. The infinitival clause in the above examples can be taken together as the complement. In other words, they function as inherent complement verbs because they take predicative structures as in: ị̀'fụ́ ńnà yá; ị̀'zà ụ́nọ̀; and í'bídó ọ́lụ́. The entire predicative clause is the complement of the first clause.

4.1.2 The Participle

The participle in Ọnịcha dialect of Igbo is a verbal derivative which is always preceded by an auxiliary verb – whether primary or modal auxiliary. In Ọnịcha Igbo, the participle has the morpheme constituent CV radical (verb root) and a derivational harmonizing vowel prefix *a-/e-/ẹ-* according to the vowel of the verb root.

Many dynamic and stative verbs in Ọnịcha Igbo yield the derivatives called participle. It is formed by affixing a harmonizing vowel prefix to the verb root, as in:

PREFIX	VERB ROOT	PARTICIPLE
ẹ-	-vb: jẹ́ *go*	ẹ-vb: èjẹ́ *going*
a-	-vb: zà *sweep*	a-vb: ázà *sweeping*
e-	-vb: sí *cook*	e-vb: èsí *cooking*

Table 4-IX The formation of the Ọnịcha participle

The participle, like the infinitive, is a nomino-verbal because it has attributes, both of the noun and of the verb. It is normally used with its complement and it is the only verbal derivative that takes inflectional affixes. For instance, in Ọnịcha Igbo, the participle can take the perfective suffix =*go* to yield a perfective participle, as in:

    36. èlígó   *has/have eaten*
    37. ázàgó   *has/have swept*
    38. àlụ́gó   *has/have worked*
    39. ákọ̀gó   *has/have planted*

Affixation and Auxiliaries in Igbo

As regards tones, for simple participle, the prefix is low for high tone verbs, and high for low tone verbs, as in the following examples:

40	Àdá nà-*àzụ́* á'fị́á Ada aux-*participle* market progr. *trading* Ada is trading/Ada is a trader
41	Íbè gà-*àsụ́gó* ákwà Ibe mod-*participle*-perf.suff cloth aux. *washing* Ibe may/must have washed clothes
42	Ńgọ́zị̂ á'*má* éjẹ́ ákwụ́kwọ́ Ngozi pref-*neg.aux* participle book going Ngozi will not go to school
43	Fà á'*dá* àkwụ́ ụ́'gwọ́ They pref-*pm.aux* participle payment paying They don't pay/They are not paying
44	Ị̀ *má* 'ésí ń'ní You(sing.) mod.aux participle food cooking You may/must not cook
45	Ọ̀ *dá* èkwú ó'kwú He/she neg.aux participle speech speaking He/she is not talking/He /she does not talk/He/she is dumb

Table 4-X Constructions with simple participle in Ọnịcha

From the foregoing examples, we observe that every participle cited above is preceded by an auxiliary, whether primary auxiliary, as in (40), (43), and (45), or modal auxiliary, as in (41), (42), and (44).

The participle can co-occur with the perfective inflectional suffix =*go*, as in (41). We observe that the perfective inflectional suffix =*go* co-occurs only with the modal auxiliary, both affirmative and negative (*ga* and *ma*) but not with the primary auxiliary (*na* and *dị*). The tone changes are as follows:

- low tone prefix for high tone verb roots
- high tone prefix for low tone verb roots

All the participles in the above examples are followed by their complements.

4.1.3 Prefixation and Reduplication

Reduplication is a term in morphology which describes a process of repetition whereby the form of a prefix/suffix reflects certain phonological characteristics of the root (Crystal 1985:259). In the Ọnịcha Igbo dialect, the prefixation and total reduplication involve the derivative morpheme ò/ọ̀, the reduplicated verb root and the verb root. Eke (1985:181) represents the process of reduplication in Ngwa as OCV_1CV_2, where:

- O represents the derivative morpheme
- CV_1 represents the reduplicated verb root
- CV_2 represents the verb root.

4.1.3a Prefixation and Total Reduplication

The total or full reduplication takes place when the onset of the verb root and its accompanying vowels are reduplicated, as in the following examples:

	DERIVATIVE MORPHEME	VERB ROOT	DERIVED NOMINAL	GLOSS
46	Ò	bí *live*	Òbíbí	*act of living*
47	Ò	bì *borrow*	Òbìbì	*act of borrowing or lending*
48	Ò	sí *cook*	Òsísí	*act of cooking*
49	Ò	kwú *speak*	Òkwúkwú	*act of speaking*
50	Ọ̀	pụ̀ *go out/leave*	ọ̀pụ̀pụ̀	*act of going out/leaving*
51	Ọ̀	mị̀ *suck/siphon*	ọ̀mị̀mị̀	*act of sucking*
52	Ọ̀	sụ́ *wash*	ọ̀sụ́sụ́	*act of washing*
53	Ọ̀	zụ̀ *train/breed*	ọ̀zụ̀zụ̀	*act of training*

Table 4-XI A schema of total reduplication in Ọnịcha

The data above show that all the vowels involved in this type of derivation are close back and close front /i/, /ị/, /u/, /ụ/ (subject to ATR harmony). The derivative morpheme is consistently low toned, and it harmonizes with the vowel of the verb root. The reduplication is said to be total or full when the verb root is integrally reduplicated. It is a very systematic and productive process of derivation in the Ọnịcha Igbo dialect.

4.1.3b Prefixation and Partial Reduplication

Partial reduplication in the Ọnịcha dialect of Igbo is the type of reduplication that takes place when the verb roots contain vowels other than those specified as [+ high], i.e. if the roots end in /e/, /a/, /ẹ/, or /o/. Such derivatives are formed by prefixing the consonant of the root to the infinitive verb form and affixing a harmonizing o-/ọ- to it, as in the following examples:

Affixation and Auxiliaries in Igbo

	DERIVATIVE MORPHEME	CONSONANT OF VERB ROOT	VERB ROOT	DERIVATIVE	GLOSS
54	Ò	-z-	-zà *sweep*	òzìzà	*act of sweeping*
55	Ò	-d-	-dà *fall*	òdìdà	*act of falling*
56	Ò	-z-	-zó *drag*	òzízó	*act of dragging*
57	Ò	-k-	-kò *plant*	òkìkò	*act of planting*
58	Ò	-t-	-tá *chew*	òtítá	*act of chewing*
59	Ò	-j-	-jé *go*	òjíjé	*act of going*
60	Ò	-w-	-wè *take*	òwìwè	*act of taking*
61	Ò	-ch-	-chó *search*	òchíchó	*act of searching*
62	Ò	-y-	-yò *sift*	òyìyò	*act of sifting*

Table 4-XII Partial reduplication in Ọnịcha

The above data show that the derivative morpheme o-/ọ- of the partial reduplicative derivative is consistently low-toned, just as in the total reduplicated derivative. There is consistency in the formation of the derivative as the consonant of the verb root is always prefixed to the infinitive form. The derivative from both the total reduplication and the partial reduplication are referred to as the *verbal noun* by Williamson (1972).

4.1.4 Prefixation and Suffixation

Prefixation and suffixation as derivational processes in Ọnịcha Igbo are characterized by the affixation of both prefix and suffix to the same base to derive a new word. Though the process involves prefixation and suffixation, it is quite distinct from circumfixation. This is because each derivative is peculiar to itself, and the prefix and suffix frame does not serve as a mould where other elements can fit in to derive other words, as in Ejele (1996:84), where *u...min* serves as a circumfixal frame for the derivation of nominals in Esan. In Igbo, the structural frame for derivation through prefixation and suffixation is P-VR-S, where:

- P = prefix
- VR = verb root, which loses part of its original semantic content as verb
- S = suffix

For the sake of simplicity and clarity, we shall group the derivatives from prefixation and suffixation in Ọnịcha into three, according to their morphological structures.

Group A   -   Derived Nominals

	VERB ROOT	PREFIX	SUFFIX	DERIVATIVE	
63	-kà *mark*	Á	Là	á-kà-là	*sign*
64	-sị *say*	À	lị	à-sị-lị	*gossip*
65	-kpé *pray*	ẹ́	lẹ	ẹ̀-kpé-lẹ́	*prayer*
66	-kwò *be envious*	E	Lo	é-kwò-lò	*envy*

	VERB ROOT		PREFIX	SUFFIX	DERIVATIVE	
67	-ghẹ́	yawn	U	lẹ	ú-ghẹ́-'lẹ́	a yawn
68	-zẹ́	sneeze	U	lẹ	ú-zẹ́-'lẹ́	a sneeze
69	-kwà	cough	U	La	ụ́-kwá-là	a cough
70	-ghẹ́	open	ọ	lẹ	ọ́-'ghẹ́-lẹ́	small opening
71	-lò	think	I	Lo	ì-lò-lò	thought

Table 4-XIII Derivation through prefixation and suffixation I

Group B   -   Derived Nominals

	VERB ROOT		PREFIX	SUFFIX	DERIVATIVE
72	-chè	think	ẹ	chẹ	ẹ́-chì-chè
73	-jú	ask	a	ju	á-jù-jú
74	-zá	answer	a	Za	á-zì-zá
75	-bó	accuse	e	bo	é-bù-bó
76	-jẹ̀	imitate		Ji	ẹ́-jì-jẹ́

Table 4-XIV Derivation through prefixation and suffixation II

Group C   -   Derived Nominals and Adjectives

	VERB ROOT		PREFIX	SUFFIX	DERIVATIVE
77	-gbọ	vomit	A	ọ	á-gbọ́-'ọ́
78	-gụ	hunger/be hungry	A	ụ	á-gụ́-'ụ́
79	-kpọ́	dry	ọ	ọ	ọ́-kpọ́-'ọ́
80	-jọ́	be ugly	ọ	ọ	ọ́-jọ́-'ọ́
81	-jọ́	be bad	A	ọ	á-jọ́-'ọ́
82	-jí	be black	O	I	ó-jí-'í

Table 4-XV Derivation through prefixation and suffixation III

Considering the three groups of derivatives, it is observed that groups A and B are nominals and they have their suffixes as =LV where L is a consonant and V any vowel. In group A, the suffixal consonant is consistently 'L', while the vowel of the suffix is the same as that of the verb root. In group B, the suffixal consonant is the consonant of the verb root, while the vowel of the suffix is also the vowel of the verb root. In other words, the suffix of group B is a reduplication of the verb root. This is, however, not the same as partial reduplication that we have discussed above. In group C, the suffixes are all vowels. These vowels are the extensions of the vowels of the verb roots. We observe in group C that some derivatives are nominals, while some may be used as adjectives. They are old formations that are no longer productive. Infact, these formations are probably lost in history.

4.2 Interfixation

Interfixation is a process of derivation whereby an affix occurs between two identical or, sometimes, non-identical roots. In other words, an interfix interrupts the sequence of two roots. Igbo interfixes are morphemes which perform distinct derivational functions such that nouns can be derived from nouns or from verbs. The interfixes are either consonants or monosyllabic CV forms and, as the name implies, they are found between two roots.

In Ọnịcha Igbo, the most prominent interfixes are: -m-, -t-, -n-, -li-, -ta-, for noun-base form of derivatives, while –m- and –l- are common in the verb base form of derivatives. The structural pattern of derivations involving interfixes in Ọnịcha Igbo is: VP-VR-I-VP-VR where:

- VP = verbal prefix
- VR = verb root
- I = interfix etc.

We shall distinguish noun-base form of interfixation from verb-base form. In the noun-base form, the derivation is from noun to noun with no verbal prefix, while in the verb-base, the derivation stems from the verb with the corresponding verbal prefix. In other words, the structural pattern for interfixal derivation given above does not apply to the noun-base form of interfixation.

4.2.1 The Noun-Base Form of Interfixation
Anagbọgụ (1990:42) describes this derivation as old formation, idiosyncratic, irregular, and unproductive. He cites the following examples:

	BASE (NOUN)		INTERFIX	DERIVATION	GLOSS
83	ánụ́	meat	-m-	ánụ́mànụ̀	beast, animal
84	ụ̀wà	world	-t-	ụ̀wàtụ́wà	Generation
85	ó'gó	height	-n-	Ógónógó	Tallness
86	m̀pẹ́	small	-li-	ḿpẹ́lị́ḿpẹ́	little bits
87	ńgọ̀	a bend	-li-	ńgọ̀lị́ńgọ̀	Crookedness
88	ḿkpú anthill		-ta-	ḿkpụ́táḿkpụ́	elevation, uneven ground

Table 4-XVI *The noun-base form of interfixation*

Following Anagbọgụ, we observe that the above noun-base form of interfixation is indeed irregular and does not require any prefix, thereby transgressing the structural pattern of derivation given above. The pattern for the noun-base derivation is rather N-I-N, where:

- N = noun
- I = interfix

We observe also that the examples given by Anagbọgụ are also applicable to Ọnịcha Igbo.

4.2.2 The Verb-Base Form of Interfixation

The verb base derivatives have the verb as their base form for deriving nominals. They follow the interfixational structural pattern of derivation shown above. In what follows, we shall present the examples in two stages. The first stage comprises examples of -m- interfixes followed by examples of -l- interfixes in the second stage.

a. The –m- Interfix

	BASE (VERB)		INTERFIX	DERIVATIVE	GLOSS
89	Lí	eat	-m-	Élímélí	*Banquet/Feast*
90	Sí	cook	-m-	Ésímésí	*Cookery*
91	Mù̩	learn	-m-	ámù̩màmù̩	*Education*
92	kpú̩	mould	-m-	ákpú̩mákpú̩	*Sculpture*
93	Bà	enter	-m-	Ábàmàbà	*Entry*
94	tù̩	point out	-m-	átù̩màtù̩	*Example*
95	gú̩	read/count	-m-	águ̩mágú̩	*Studies*
96	Kwú	speak/talk	-m-	ékwúmékwú	*Speech*

Table 4-XVII The verb-base form on interfixation – the -m- interfix

Examples above show that the interfix -m- links together two verb roots to form a nominal derivative. There is a close semantic affinity between the verb roots and the derivatives. The tone of the derivatives is the same as that of the verb root, for both high and low tone verb roots; for instance, a high tone verb root yields a derivative that has all its tones as high, while a low tone verb root yields a low tone derivative except for the prefix, which, in both high and low tone verb roots, remains consistently high.

b. The -l- Interfix

The following are examples of derivatives formed with the **-l-** interfix.

	BASE (VERB)		INTERFIX	DERIVATIVE	GLOSS
97	kwú	speak	-l-	èkwúlèkwú	*Talkativeness*
98	gwù	play	-l-	égwùlé'gwú	*a play*
99	fù	to get lost	-l-	Éfùléfù	*Prodigality*
100	kú̩	mix	-l-	àkù̩làkú̩	*an unholy mixture*
101	ká	to be worn	-li̩-	ńkáli̩ńká	*Tattered*
102	gò	to be bent	-li̩-	ńgòli̩ǹgò	*Tortuous*
103	chó̩	to be tiny	-li̩-	ńchó̩li̩ńchó̩	*extremely tiny*
104	pé̩	to be small	-li̩-	ḿpé̩li̩ḿpé̩	*Smallishness*

Table 4-XVIII The verb-base form of interfixation – the -l- interfix

From the above examples, it is observed that the prefix is high for some low tone verb roots and low for some high tone verb roots, save for some exceptional cases where the prefixes are syllabic nasals. There is also a tonal modification in (100) where the verb root is a high tone, and, at the derived form, both the prefix and the root are reduced to low tones.

We observe also that when the derivative has a vowel prefix, the interfix is a single morpheme -l-, but when the prefix is a syllabic nasal, the interfix is CV.
In actual utterance, the derivatives with syllabic nasal prefixes are shortened so that the actual realization is as follows:

- ńkị́lị́ká for ńkálị́ńká
- ǹgò̩ńgò̩ for ǹgò̩lị́ǹgò̩
- ńchó̩ńchó̩ for ńchó̩lị́ńchó̩
- ḿpé̩ḿpé̩ for ḿpé̩lị́ḿpé̩

Both realizations are possible in Ọnịcha, but native speakers prefer the abridged form since it does not affect the meaning of the words.

4.3 Circumfixation
Ndimele (1999:33) quoting Allerton (1979) defines circumfixation as a situation where both the prefix and the suffix are simultaneously employed to express one meaning. The circumfix is a discontinuous morpheme which surrounds the root of a word such that the first half occurs before the root and the second half occurs after the root.

In Ọnịcha Igbo, the circumfix is used to derive nominals from verbs. The derivation is formed by inserting the baseform or the verb root into the circumfixal frame (or paradigm) *a/e...mu*. The following examples explicate the circumfixation in Ọnịcha.

	BASE FORM/VERB ROOT	CIRCUMFIX	DERIVATIVE	GLOSS
105	lí *eat*	e…mu	èlímúńní/ èlímńní	*act of eating*
106	sụ́ *wash*	a…mu	àsụ́mụ́ákwà/àsụ́ mákwà	*act of washing*
107	zú *trade*	a…mu	àzúmáfị́á	*act of trading*
108	bẹ́ á'kwá *cry*	ẹ…mu	ẹ̀bẹ́mákwá	*act of crying*
109	kwụ́ ọ́'tọ́ *stand*	a…mu	àkwụ́mọ́tọ́	*act of standing*

Table 4-XIX Circumfixation in Ọnịcha

Circumfixation is a very productive process and can be used to derive many of life's experiences in Ọnịcha. Ọnịcha circumfixes differ from those of other languages like Esan and Eleme in the sense that the circumfixes in Ọnịcha must co-occur with their verbal complements.

4.4 Deverbatives

Deverbatives are nominals which are derived directly from verbs (Ndimele 2003:64). They have morphological resemblance to the verb root from which they are derived. As nominals, deverbatives can serve as minimal subject NPs, objects, or complements of verbs. Deverbatives in Ọnịcha Igbo variety will be discussed under the following headings:

- Bound Cognate Noun (BCN)
- Gerund (simple and complex)
- Noun agent (agentives)
- Noun instrument (instrumentals)
- Noun of Result (qualificatives)
- Miscellaneous/non-productive deverbatives

We shall now discuss the above one by one.

4.4.1 The Bound Cognate Noun (BCN)

The Bound Cognate Noun, (henceforth BCN), is, according to Emenanjo (1978:132), one of the nominal and complementary elements of the Igbo verb. It is a verbal derivative which is always used bound to and after the verb from which it is derived. The BCN is formed by affixing the harmonizing low tone verbal vowel prefix a=/e=/ẹ= to the verb stem. It is more associated with activity verbs than with statives in the Ọnịcha dialect of Igbo. We shall, in what follows, give examples of BCN in constructions; this will be done in three stages using the same set of sentences. It will enable us capture the functions of Igbo complement and BCN respectively. The examples will be presented in the following order:

a. sentences with both NP complement and BCN.
b. sentences with NP complement only (without BCN).
c. sentences with BCN only (without complement).

a.   Sentences with Both NP Complement and BCN

110	N'nẹ	sì*lì*	ńní	'ésí
	Mother	vb-*LV*	NP comp.	BCN
		cook-*FT*	food	cooking
	Mother actually cooked the food			
111	Àdá	kwà*lù*	ákwà	àkwá
	Ada	vb-*LV*	NP comp.	BCN
		sew-*FT*	cloth	sewing
	Ada actually sewed the cloth			
112	Ànyị	gbà*lù*	égwú	'ágbá
	We	vb-*LV*	NP comp.	BCN
		dance-*FT*	dance	dancing
	We actually did/performed/danced the dance			

Affixation and Auxiliaries in Igbo

113	Fá	kò*lù*		ẹ́dẹ̀	àkọ̀
	They	vb-*LV*		NP comp.	BCN
		plant-*FT*		cocoyam	planting
	They actually planted the cocoyam				
114	Ọ́	zà*lù*		ụ́nọ̀	àzà
	He/she	vb-*LV*		NP comp.	BCN
		sweep-*FT*		house	sweeping
	He/she actually swept the house				

Table 4-XX Constructions with both NP complement and BCN

b. Sentences with NP Complement Only (without BCN)

115	Ń'nẹ́	sì*lì*	ńní
	Nne	vb-*LV*	NP compl.
		cook-*FT*	food
	Nne cooked food		
116	Àdá	kwà*lù*	ákwà
	Ada	vb-*LV*	NP compl.
		sew-*FT*	cloth
	Ada sewed the cloth		
117	Ànyí	gbà*lù*	égwú
	We	vb-*LV*	NP compl.
		dance-*FT*	dance
	We danced		
118	Fá	kò*lù*	ẹ́dẹ̀
	They	vb-*LV*	NP compl.
		plant-*FT*	cocoyam
	They planted cocoyam		
119	Ọ́	zà*lù*	ụ́nọ̀
	He/she	vb-*LV*	NP compl.
		sweep-*FT*	house
	He/she swept the house		

Table 4-XXI Constructions with NP complement only – BCN

c. Sentences with BCN Only

120	Ń'nẹ́	sìlì	èsí
	Nne	cooked	cooking
121	Àdá	kwàlù	àkwá
	Ada	sewed	sewing
122	Ànyí	gbàlù	àgbá
	We	ran	running
123	Fá	kòlù	àkọ̀
	They	planted	planting

124	Ọ́	zàlụ̀	àzà
	He/she	swept	sweeping

Table 4-XXII Constructions with BCN only

With reference to the three sets of sentences above, it is observed that sentences in (a) and (b) are grammatical and acceptable in Ọnịcha Igbo dialect. They express exactly the same thing except that in (a) the sentences are uttered with more emphasis, as shown above by the presence of the BCN. In (b), the sentences are mere statements of fact. They are indicative statements; they simply express the roles of the arguments – the agent and the patient – without the emphasis of the (a) sentences.

In (c), the sentences cannot be understood without the listener knowing beforehand the context of the discussion. It is only the context that gives the expressions their semantic value. The (a) and (b) groups of sentences above are typical examples of normal Ọnịcha Igbo sentences. The (b) group of sentences is as grammatical as the (a) group, showing that the complement is more syntactically pertinent in the Ọnịcha Igbo sentences than the BCN, the BCN serving solely as an emphatic element. The conclusion that can be deduced from the above examples is that Ọnịcha Igbo sentences can do without BCN, but may not always do without the complement. We can schematically represent the co-occurrence of BCN and complement as follows:

- NP + V + Complement [+ BCN] → semantically full + emphasis
- NP + V + Complement [- BCN] → semantically full – emphasis
- NP + V - Complement [+ BCN] → semantically incomplete without context
- NP + V - Complement [+ BCN] + context → semantically full

The above confirms the claim that sentences in (c) are context-bound. The deletion of BCN from the other sentences will affect neither the grammaticality nor the acceptability of the sentences. We observe from the above examples that the BCN occurs in the adverbial slot in all the constructions.

Morphologically, the BCN is closer to its verb than the complement, but semantically, the complement is closer to its verb than the BCN. It then means that the syntactic function and the semantic interpretation that can be assigned to the BCN are contextually determined.

In isolation, the complement can be specified as an independent lexical item (e.g. *ńní, ákwà, égwú, ụ́nọ̀, ú'gbó*) but the BCN cannot be so specified because it is a verb-bound element whose meaning is contextually determined. We can therefore argue that the BCN can never occur independent of the verb to which it is morphologically and semantically related.

4.4.2 Gerunds

A gerund is a nominal element that is derived from a verb base. Gerunds are mostly formed from active verbs. Williamson (1972) refers to a gerund as a verbal noun. Gerunds are of two distinct types – simple and complex gerunds.

The simple gerunds are formed from simple verb roots, while the complex gerunds are formed from complex verb roots. Simple gerunds have earlier been examined under the section Prefixation and Reduplication (Ref. 4.1.3).

The complex gerund has a homorganic syllabic nasal prefix affixed to the base form of the verb. The following are examples of complex gerunds formed from both disyllabic and trisyllabic verb roots.

	SYLLABIC NASAL	BASE VERB ROOT	COMPLEX VERB	INFINITIVE	DERIVED GERUND	GLOSS
125	m	bú *carry*	búbà *carry in*	íbūbà *to carry in*	m̄búbà	*act of carrying in*
126	m	bá *spread*	básà *spread out*	íbāsà *to spread out*	m̄básà	*act of spreading out*
127	m	bẹ̀ *cut*	bẹ́pụ̀ *cut off*	íbẹ̄pụ̀ *to cut off*	m̄bẹ́pụ̀	*act of cutting off*
128	n	dà *fall*	dápụ̀ *fall off*	ídāpụ̀ *to fall off*	ńdápụ̀	*act of falling off*
129	ŋ	gbá *run*	gbápụ̀ *run off*	ígbāpụ̀ *to run off*	ŋ́gbápụ̀	*act of running off*
130	n	kọ́ *narrate*	kọ́chá *criticize*	íkọ̄chā *to criticize*	ńkọ́chá	*act of criticizing*
131	ŋ	kọ́ *plant*	kọ̀chà *scoop*	íkọ̀chà *to scoop (out)*	ńkọ̀chá	*act of scooping (out)*
132	ŋ	kwú *stand*	kwúpụ̀tá *stand out*	íkwūpụ̀tà *to stand out*	ŋkwúpụ̀tá	*act of standing out*
133	n	zà *sweep*	zápụ̀ *sweep out*	ízāpụ̀ *to sweep out*	ńzápụ̀	*act of sweeping out*
134	n	tụ́ *throw*	túfù *throw away*	ítūfù *to throw away*	Ńtúfù	*act of throwing away*

Table 4-XXIII Complex Gerunds in Ọnịcha

From the foregoing examples, it is observed that the derivative morpheme for a complex gerund is a homorganic syllabic nasal prefix m (bilabial), and n (dental and alveolar). This contrasts with the derivative morpheme of a simple gerund, which is a low-toned harmonizing back vowel prefix ò-/ọ̀-. The root of a simple gerund is a single verb, while that of a complex gerund is a compound or a complex verb root. A consistency is observed in the tonal behaviour of the syllabic nasal in the derivation of a complex gerund. For instance, the syllabic nasal prefix is high in all the derivatives as opposed to the derivative morpheme prefix in the derivation of simple gerund which is consistently low.

4.4.3 The Noun Agent

The noun agent, otherwise termed agentive, denotes the doer of something. Ndimele (2003:70), quoting Comrie and Thompson (1985:351), defines agentive as *one which verbs*. In the Ọnịcha dialect of Igbo, the noun agent is formed by prefixing a harmonizing derivational low tone morpheme ò-/ọ̀- to the basic form of the verb. The structural pattern of the agentive in Ọnịcha Igbo is as follows: *ò-VR* where ò = a harmonizing open back vowel prefix and VR = the verb root.

The following are some examples of noun agent in the Ọnịcha dialect of Igbo.

	AGENTIVE MORPHEME	VERB ROOT	DERIVED NOMINAL	COMPLEMENT OF NOUN	DERIVED NA + COMPLEMENT	GLOSS
135	Ò	sí *cook*	ò-sí *cook*	ńní *food*	òsí 'ńní	*Cook*
136	Ò	gbú *kill*	ò-gbú *killer*	ánụ́ *meat*	ògbú 'ánụ́	*butcher*
137	Ò	kwú *speak*	ò-kwú *speaker*	ókwú *word*	òkwú 'ókwú	*speaker*
138	Ọ̀	dẹ́ *write*	ọ̀-dẹ́ *writer*	ákwụ́kwọ́ *book*	ọ̀dẹ́ 'ákwụ́kwọ́	*secretary*
139	Ọ̀	jé *go*	ò-jé *goer*	ózí *message*	òjé 'ózí	*messenger*
140	Ọ̀	zụ́ *trade*	ọ̀-zụ́ *trader*	áfị́á *market*	ọ̀zụ́ 'áfị́á	*trader*
141	Ọ̀	zà *sweep*	ọ̀-zá *sweeper*	ụ̀nọ̀ *house*	ọ̀zá ụ̀nọ̀	*cleaner*
142	Ọ̀	sụ́ *clear*	ọ̀-sụ́ *cutter*	ófị́á *bush*	ọ̀sụ́ 'ófị́á	*labourer*
143	Ọ̀	sụ́ *wash*	ọ̀-sụ́ *washer*	ákwà *cloth*	ọ̀sụ́ àkwà	*washerman*
144	Ọ̀	kọ̀ *plant*	ọ̀-kọ́ *sower*	ú'gbó *farm*	ọ̀kọ́ úgbó	*farmer*
145	Ọ̀	sá *wash*	ọ̀-sá *washer*	áfẹ́lẹ́ *plate*	ọ̀sá 'áfẹ́lẹ́	*dishwasher*

Table 4-XXIV Noun agents in Ọnịcha

From the above data, it is observed that there is tonal modification in the derivatives of the noun agents. The high tone of the noun complement is consistently lowered to a downstep when preceded by the high tone verb roots. The derivative morpheme ò-/ọ̀- has a low tone in all the examples, while the vowel of the root has a high tone. It is observed that the noun complement with a high-low tone is lowered to a low-low tone in the derived form as in ọ̀zá ụ̀nọ̀ *house sweeper*. There is vowel harmony in operation between the derivative morpheme and the verb root.

Apart from expressing the doer of something, the derived agentive can be used perjoratively, either to ridicule or humiliate someone, especially when it is used in isolation without the affected entity or the complement. Ndimele (2003:71) describes such agentives that convey perjorative meaning as *derisive agentives*. Examples of such derisive agentives in Ọnịcha Igbo are:

	D.M.	VERB ROOT	SUFFIX	DERIVATIVES	GLOSS
146	Ọ̀	jẹ́ *go*	gọ̀	ọ̀jẹ́gọ̀	has to do with the verb *go*
147	Ọ̀	sí *cook*	gọ̀	ọ̀sígọ̀	has to do with the verb *cook*
148	Ọ̀	lụ́ *work*	gọ̀	ọ̀lụ́gọ̀	has to do with the verb *work*
149	Ọ̀	dẹ́ *write*	gọ̀	ọ̀dẹ́gọ̀	has to do with the verb *write*
150	Ọ̀	zá *sweep*	gọ̀	ọ̀zágọ̀	has to do with the verb *sweep*
151	Ọ̀	kọ́ *plant*	gọ̀	ọ̀kọ́gọ̀	has to do with the verb *plant/farm*

Table 4-XXV Derisive agentives in Ọnịcha

In each of the above examples, the agentive is used sarcastically and the sarcastic element is *-gọ̀* which is constant in all the examples. From the vowel harmony point of view, it is also invariable. Emenanjo (1978:156) affirms that this type of derivative is used alone in one-word utterances, especially when sarcasm is intended.

4.4.4 The Noun Instrument

The noun instrument (NI) denotes the instrument with which something is done. It is a nominal element that is derived from a verb base through some derivational processes. Ndimele (2003:72) refers to it as *instrumental*. It is formed by prefixing a low tone homorganic nasal to the verb root. In some cases, the instruments require their own complement in order to be structurally and semantically complete. The following are some of the examples of noun instruments in Ọnịcha Igbo.

	VERB ROOT	DERIVED NOUN INSTRUMENT	NOUN COMPLEMENT	DERIVED (NI) + COMPLEMENT	GLOSS
152	gbú *kill*	m̀gbú	ọ̀kẹ́	m̀gbú'ọ́kẹ́	*rat killer/poison*
153	gwú *dig*	ŋ̀gwú	ànì	ŋ̀gwúànì	*Digger*
154	kpọ́ *drive into ground*	ŋ̀kpọ́	Ànì	ŋ̀kpọ́nànì	*Cannon*

	VERB ROOT	DERIVED NOUN INSTRUMENT	NOUN COMPLEMENT	DERIVED (NI) + COMPLEMENT	GLOSS
155	yọ̀ *sift*	ǹyọ̀	á'kpụ́	ǹyọ̀ á'kpụ́	*cassava sieve*
156	zà *filter*	ǹzà	ọ́gwụ̀	ǹzà ọ́gwụ̀	*drug sieve*
157	rá *comb*	ǹrá	ísí	ǹrá 'ísí	*hair comb*
158	tẹ́ *scrub*	ǹtẹ́	ụ́nọ̀	ǹtẹ́tẹ́ ụ́nọ̀	*local paintbrush*
159	Kọ̀ *cultivate*	ŋ̀kọ̀		ŋ̀kọ̀	*farm implement*

Table 4-XXVI *Noun instruments in Ọnịcha*

From the foregoing examples, a sort of consistency is observed in the tonal behaviour of the derived NI and the derived NI plus the complement. For instance, all the homorganic nasal prefixes have low tones. The high tone verb roots maintain their high tone in the derived noun instrument, and also in the derived noun instrument plus complement. The low tone verb roots also maintain their low tone in the derived noun instrument and in the derived noun instrument plus complement. The complements are inherent to some of the derived noun instruments.

For instance, -kpọ́ *drive into ground* has a fixed or narrow collocational range because it can only co-occur with *ground* so that the derived noun instrument plus the complement is ŋ̀kpọ́nànị̀. -yọ̀, on the other hand, has a wide collocational range because it co-occurs with all elements that are sievable. Such elements may be powdery, granular, or in solid form, as in ǹyọ̀ á'kpụ́ *cassava sieve*; cassava may be in solid, fermented, wet form; it can also be in powdered form as dry, ground, cassava flour. -yọ́ can also co-occur with the following complements:

    160.   ǹyọ̀ ọ́kà   *maize sieve*
    161.   ǹyọ̀ á'kpụ́   *cassava sieve*
    162.   ǹyọ́ gàrí   *garri sieve*

-gwú *dig* can have narrow, but not fixed collocational restriction when in a derived form. It co-occurs with ànị̀ *ground* when it refers to a professional digger, but it can also co-occur with jí *yam* when it refers to the digging implement specifically used in the harvesting of yam. –gwú can therefore be realized as derived noun instrument, as in:

    163.   ŋ̀gwú ànị̀   *digger*
    164.   ŋ̀gwú 'jí   *yam digger*

-kọ̀ *plant* can only exist as ŋ̀kọ̀ without complement. It is a farm implement used mostly for weeding.

-gbú *kill* has a wide collocational range when it serves to derive a noun instrument m̀gbú, as in:

165.	m̀gbú 'ọ́kẹ́	*rat killer/poison*
166.	m̀gbú 'ágwọ́	*snake killer/poison*

-zà *filter* is similar to -yò *sift/sieve* in the sense that both elements suggest the separation of solids or coarse materials from liquids or finer particles. ǹzà or ǹyọ̀ is constructed with perforated material. The difference between ǹyọ̀ and ǹzà is that ǹyọ̀ co-occurs mostly with solid substances which can be dry or wet. Ǹzà co-occurs mostly with liquids, as in:

167.	ǹzà ọ́gwù̀	*drug filter*
168.	ǹzà ḿmí'lí	*water filter*

ǹyọ̀ and ǹzà can be differentiated, thus:

- ǹyọ̀ = ± solid
- ǹzà = - solid

The following are unacceptable in Ọnịcha Igbo:

169.	*ǹyọ̀ ḿmí'lí
170.	*ǹzà á'kpụ́
171.	*ǹyọ̀ 'jí

-rá *comb* has a fixed collocational range in its derived form ǹrá *a comb*. It can only co-occur with the complement ísí *head* as ǹrá 'ísí *hair comb*.

4.4.5 The Noun of Result

The Noun of Result indicates the action or state resulting from the verb. It is formed by prefixing a low tone homorganic syllabic nasal to the base form of the verb. The derivative can be formed with either activity or stative verbs. When the verb is stative, the Noun of Result functions as the nominal complement of its verb. But when the verb is an activity verb, the derivative may be used to qualify the complement of the verb. This may have informed the term *qualificative* as used by Ndimele (2003:74) to refer to the same Noun of Result. He describes qualificatives (Nouns of Result) as verbal derivatives which have adjectival attributes because they can specify or limit the reference of nominals. The following are some examples of Nouns of Result:

	VERB ROOT		SN	DERIVED NOUN OF RESULT
172	-mẹ́	*do*	m̀	m̀mẹ́ *the result of doing*
173	-tụ́ í'mé	*be pregnant*	ǹ	ǹtụ́ í'mé *the result of being pregnant*
174	-jí	*be black*	ǹ	ǹjí *the result of being black/blackness*
175	-pẹ́	*be small*	m̀	m̀pẹ́ *the result of being small/smallness*
176	-jọ́	*be ugly*	ń	ńjọ́ *the result of being ugly/ugliness*
177	-má	*be fine/beautiful*	ḿ	ḿ'má *the result of being beautiful/beauty*

Table 4-XXVII Nouns of result in Ọnịcha

It is observed that the Nouns of Result are few in the dialect. Many of them are formed from stative verbs, as in:

178. i̱'jó ńjó   *to be ugly/to be wicked*
179. i̱'jí ńjí/ójí   *to be black*
180. i̱'má ḿ'má   *to be beautiful*

The above nominal elements can be found in NP subject postions, as in the following sentences:

181	Ńjó	nwáànyí	à	dì	égwù
	Ugliness	woman	this	be	fear
	This woman's ugliness is terrible					

Table 4-XXVIII Noun of result in NP subject position

Ńjó can also be found in NP object position as in:

182	Nwáànyí	à	jò*lù*	ńjó
	Woman	this	vb-*LV*	ugliness
			be ugly-*ST*	
	This woman is ugly				

Table 4-XXIX Noun of result in NP object position

Note that ńjó cannot be confused with ǹjó as has been explained earlier because ǹjó means *sin*, whereas ńjó means *ugliness*. The semantic link between the two of them is the underlying notion of *badness* that exists in both.

Ḿ'má and ǹjí can also be realized as both NP subject and NP object, as in the following:

183	Ḿ'má	'yá	gwù*lù*	àkù
	Beauty	him/her	vb-*LV*	wealth
			finish-*FT*	
	Her beauty cost a lot				

Table 4-XXX M'ma in NP subject position

184	Ó	mà*lù*	ḿmá	dí	égwù
	He/she	vb-*LV*	beauty	be	fear
		be beautiful-*ST*			
	He/she is extremely beautiful					

Table 4-XXXI M'ma in NP object position

185	Ǹjí/Òjí	Ádá	nà-ámụ̀kẹ́sị́	àmụ̀kẹ́sị́
	Blackness	Ada	aux.-pref-*vb* prog. *shine*	shining
	Ada's blackness is glistening			

Table 4-XXXII Ǹjí/òjí in NP subject position

186	Àdá	dị̀	ézígbó'ójí	black
	Ada	be	adj. good	black
	Ada is very black			

Table XXXIII Òjí in NP object position

4.4.6 Miscellaneous Deverbatives

The above term is borrowed from Ndimele (2003:75) to refer to deverbatives which manifest some unique peculiarities/irregularities in their morpho-tonemic and morpho-phonemic behaviour. Our discussion of deverbatives has been a regular and systematic process of deriving nominals from verb bases. In the present section, we shall examine deverbatives whose processes of derivation are irregular and non-systematic. Each of the derivatives is unique and should be considered separately from the others. There is no generalization as regards their method of derivation from their bases just as we have observed all along with earlier deverbatives that are regular and systematic in their formation. Ndimele says that such derivatives in Echie are no longer productive. In Ọnịcha Igbo, however, such derivatives are still numerous and they are characterized by the following:

- incoherence and heterogeneous derivative morpheme
- tonal modification
- diverse semantic interpretation
-

We shall, in what follows, group the miscellaneous derivatives together using their derivative morpheme as criterion for their grouping.

Derivative morpheme (vowel prefix a)

	VERB BASE		DERIVED NOMINAL	
187	-bụ̀	*sing*	ábụ̀	*song*
188	-dà	*fall*	ádá	*a fall*
189	-kwá	*cry*	ákwá	*a cry*
190	-kwá	*sew*	ákwà	*cloth*
191	-mụ́	*laugh*	ámụ́	*laughter*
192	-sị́	*say/tell*	àsị́	*lies*

Table 4-XXXIV Miscellaneous deverbatives with vowel prefix a

It is observed that there is consistency in the morpho-phonemic behaviour of the above derivatives. For instance, all the vowels are non-expanded and they harmonize with the vowel of the base. The tones of the derived nominals copy the tones of the verb root except in (188). The derived nominal in (188) is cognate with the verb root, while that in (189) is not.

Derivative morpheme (vowel prefix e)

	VERB ROOT		DERIVED NOMINAL	
193	-fù	*get lost*	èfù	*lost*
194	-wù	*be famous*	èwù	*fame*
195	-zù	*be complete*	èzù	*complete*

Table 4-XXXV Miscellaneous deverbatives with vowel preix e

It is observed that the above nominals have the status of inherent complements. They are all expanded vowels and the tones – both those of the base and those of the derived nominals – are the same.

Derivative morpheme (vowel prefix i)

	VERB ROOT		DERIVED NOMINAL	
196	-bú	*carry*	íbú	*load*
197	-bù	*be fat*	íbù	*fatness*
198	-kpẹ́	*judge*	í'kpé	*case/judgment*
199	-jẹ́	*go*	íjè	*a walk*
200	-nù	*be bitter*	ínú	*bitterness*
201	-sì	*smell*	ísì	*stench/odor/aroma*

Table 4-XXXVI Miscellaneous deverbatives with vowel prefix i

From the above data, it is observed that all the vowels of the derived nominals are expanded, even when the vowel of the base is a non-expanded vowel, as in (198) and (199). This confirms our earlier finding that in the Ọnịcha dialect, the vowel (200) cannot occur as a unique vowel in a monosyllabic or disyllabic lexeme but can co-occur with a nominal or verbal as participial prefix.

Derivative morpheme (vowel prefix o)

	VERB ROOT		DERIVED NOMINAL	
202	-bí	*live*	òbí	*habitation*
203	-jí	*be black*	òjí/ǹjí	*blackness*
204	-kwú	*speak/talk*	ókwú	*speech/word*

Table 4-XXXVII Miscellaneous decerbative with vowel prefix o

From the above examples, it is observed that all the vowels are expanded – both the base and those of the derived. The derivatives copy the tone of the base.

Derivative morpheme (vowel prefix ọ)

	VERB ROOT		DERIVED NOMINAL	
205	-chá	be white	òchá	white
206	-fụ́	see	ọ́fụ̀	vision
207	-dụ́	advise	ọ́'dụ́	advice
208	-kụ̀	toil	ọ́kụ̀	wealth
209	-kọ́	scratch	ọ́kọ́	rashes
210	-kè	share	òkè	a share
211	-lụ́	work	ọ́lụ́	a job
212	-nwụ́	die	ọ́nwụ́	death
213	-ñụ̀	rejoice	ọ́ñụ̀	joy
214	-yà	be sick	ọ́yà	sickness
215	-yì	befriend	òyì	friendship/adultery

Table 4-XXXVIII Miscellaneous deverbatives with vowel prefix Ọ

From the above examples, it is observed that all the vowels, those of the base and of the derived nominals alike, are non-expanded. There is tone copying of the base by the derived nominal except in example (206) where the high tone of the base vowel is lowered in the derived. In (207), the high tone of the base vowel is lowered to a step tone in the derived form.

Derivative morpheme (vowel prefix ụ)

	VERB ROOT		DERIVED NOMINAL	
216	-bá	be rich	ụ̀bá	wealth
217	-bụ́	grab	ụ̀bụ́	a grab
218	-dị́	be	ụ̀dụ́	resemblance
219	-fụ́	pain	ụ̀fụ́	pain
220	-kà	say	ụ̀kà	mass/service/discussion
221	-kọ́	be scarce	ụ̀kọ́	scarcity
222	-ná	go home	ụ̀ná	departure (for one's home)
223	-sà	to open (the palm)	ụ̀sà	intemperance
224	-sọ́	be sweet	ụ̀sọ́	sweetness
225	-tọ́	be sweet	ụ̀tọ́	sweetness

Table 4-XXXIX Miscellaneous deverbatives with vowel prefix ụ

There is consistency in the morpho-tonemic and morpho-phonemic behaviour of the above derived nominals. The vowels of the base and those of the derivative belong to the non-expanded group. The vowels of the derived nominals copy the tone of the vowels of the verb roots.

Derivative morpheme (vowel prefix u)

	VERB ROOT	DERIVED NOMINAL
226	-chè think	úchè thought

Table 4-XL Miscellaneous deverbatives with vowel prefix u

Only one example is attested in this group of morphemes. There is transformation of the vowel of the verb root from non-expanded to expanded vowel. This further confirms the former assertion that the expanded vowel 'e' in Ọnịcha does not occur in the verbal form.

Derivative morpheme (syllabic nasal prefix m)

	VERB ROOT	DERIVED NOMINAL
227	-gbá wrestle	m̀gbá wrestling
228	-gbú ache	m̀gbú ache
229	-gbụ́ be loose	m̀gbụ́ shedding leaves
230	-má be beautiful	m̄'má beauty

Table 4-XLI Miscellaneous deverbatives with prefix m

The few examples attested to in the derivation with the syllabic nasal above show that there is neat harmony between the verb roots and the derived nominals from both the morpho-tonemic and the morpho-phonemic points of view.

Derivative morpheme (syllabic nasal n)

	VERB ROOT	DERIVED NOMINAL
231	-chẹ́ guard	ǹchẹ́ watch
232	-jí be black	ǹjí blackness/darkness
233	-ká be old	ńká old age
234	-kpà tight	ǹkpà tightness
235	-kpị̀ be stingy	ǹkpị̀ miserly
236	-lọ́ dream	ńlọ́ a dream
237	-rá comb	ǹrá a comb
238	-rá pay a fine	ń'rà fine
239	-sù stammer	ǹsù stammer
240	-yọ̀ sift	ǹyọ̀ sieve
241	-zà filter	ǹzà sieve

Table 4-XLII Miscellaneous deverbatives with prefix n

From the above examples, a perfect harmony is observed between the base and the derivative from both the morpho-tonemic and morpho-phonemic points of view. The regular thing about the miscellaneous derivatives in Ọnịcha Igbo is that the derivative morpheme is a prefix which is either a vowel or a syllabic nasal and each, in its own group, has its own peculiarities.

Tone as a Derivative Morpheme in Ọnịcha Igbo

As a derivative morpheme, the tone is a non-segmental affix (super/suprafix) which can be used to perform the following functions:

- Derivation of associative relationships from determinative constructions
- Derivation of interrogative statements from declarative constructions
- derivation of nominals from sentences

i. Functions of Tone in Associative Constructions

In the associative constructions in Ọnịcha, the grammatical tones help to express possessive relationships (genitive case). The following examples are illustrative of the structures involving associative constructions:

	LEXICAL TONE					GRAMMATICAL TONE
242	Áká HH Hand		Íké HH Ike			áká 'Íké HH 'HH Ike's hand
243	àrụ́ LH Body		À'dá LH Ada	#	→	àrụ́ 'Ádá LH 'HH Ada's body
244	ụ́zọ̀ HL way/door		òkẹ́ LH Rat			ụ́'zọ́ 'ọ́kẹ́ H'H 'HH rat's way
245	ụ́nọ̀ HL House		Égō HM Ego			ụ́'nọ́ 'Égó H'H 'HH Ego's house
246	ànị̀ LL Land		Àmàlà LLL Amala			ànị́ Àmàlà LH LLL Amala's land

Table 4-XLIII Tone in associative constructions

Items from the five tone classes in Ọnịcha Igbo are combined above in associative constructions and the resultant tonal changes are summarized below as follows:

	LEXICAL TONE				GRAMMATICAL TONE
I	HH		HH		HH'HH
Ii	LH		LH		LH'HH
Iii	HL	#	LH	→	H'H'HH
Iv	HL		HM		H'H'HH
V	LL		LL		LHLL

Table 4-XLIV Summary of combination of five tone classes in Ọnịcha

From the given examples, it is observed that tonal modifications play an important role in Ọnịcha Igbo constructions. For instance, the downstep occurs when two high tones occur in succession in associative construction as in (242). The upstep occurs when a high-low tone combines or co-occurs with another low-high tone, or whenever a high-downstep tone is in association with another tone, as in (243-246) above. The lowering occurs when a high-downstep-high tone co-occurs with a high-low tone as in (245) above. What is lowered is the high tone of the first syllable in the second element of the associative construction.

ii. Functions of Tone in Determinative Constructions

In determinative constructions, the grammatical tones help to limit the reference of the constituents since they help to distinguish the modifiers from the associative tones. In other words, the tone serves as a modifier. The first element in the forthcoming examples will be referred to as the determined and the second element will be referred to as the determinant. The following are illustrative examples showing structures in determinative constructions:

	DERTERMINED	#	DETERMINANT	→	DETERMINATIVE CONSTRUCTION
247	Áká HH Hand		Íké HH Power		ákáí'ké HHH'H(downstep) high-handedness
248	Òtí LH Introducer		Ìwú LH Law		òtí'íwú LH'HH lawmaker
249	ụ́zọ̀ HL way/road	#	Àbá LH Aba	→	ụ́'zọ́ Á'bá H'H H'H(upstep) Aba road
250	ụ́nọ̀ HL House		Égō HM Money		ụ́nọ̀ é'gó HLH'H(upstep) Bank

Affixation and Auxiliaries in Igbo

	DERTERMINED	#	DETERMINANT	→	DETERMINATIVE CONSTRUCTION
251	Àkpà LL Bag		àfẹ̀ LL Dress		àkpá àfẹ̀ LHLL(upstep) dress pocket

Table 4-XLV Functions of tone in determinative constructions

The summary of the foregoing tonal modifications in determinative constructions is as follows:

i	HH		HH		HHH'H
ii	LH		LH		LH'HH
iii	HL	#	LH	→	H'HH'H
iv	HL		HM		HLH'H
v	LL		LL		LHLL

Table 4-XLVI Summary of the tonal modifications in determinative constructions

Considering the above tone rules i-v in associative and determinative constructions, it is observed that the tonal representations of associative constructions differ from those of determinative constructions, even when identical lexical tones are combined. This is because the two constructions are different. The tone in the associative construction expresses possessive construction (though not all associative constructions are possessive), while the tone in the determinative construction acts as a modifier. The functioning of tone in the two constructions as compared is shown below:

	TONES IN ASSOCIATIVE CONSTRUCTIONS					TONES IN DETERMINATIVE CONSTRUCTIONS				
i	HH		HH		HH'HH	HH		HH		HHH'H
ii	LH		LH		LH'HH	LH		LH		LHH'H
iii	HL	#	LH	→	H'H'HH	HL	#	LH	→	H'HH'H
iv	HL		HM		H'H'HH	HL		HM		HLH'H
v	LL		LL		LHLL	LL		LL		LHLL

Table 4-XLVII Tone behaviour in the associative and the determinative constructions

4.5.1 Tones in Sentences

Tone can be used in Ọnịcha Igbo to differentiate sentences or syntactic structures. Sentences which are structurally identical are differentiated semantically by their tonal modifications. For instance, interrogation is formed in Igbo by merely replacing the high tone of the subject of the declarative sentence (or the resumptive pronoun) with a low tone, as in the examples which follow:

Declarative Sentences:

252	Ọ̀ sà*lụ̀* áfẹ́lẹ́ He/she vb-*LV* plate wash-*FT* He/she washed plates
253	Fá nọ̀ n' ụ́nọ̀ They vb prep. house be in They are in the house
254	Àdá zà*lụ̀* ìló Ada vb-*LV* compound sweep-*FT* Ada swept the compound
255	Úchè sụ̀*lụ̀* ákwà Uche vb-*LV* cloth wash-*FT* Uche washed clothes
256	Íbè tò*lù* ógónógó Ibe vb-*LV* tallness be tall-*ST* Ibe is tall

Table 4-XLVIII Tone in declarative sentence constructions

The five sentences above are declarative constructions. They contain subject nouns, as in (254-256), and subject pronouns, as in (252-253). Observe the tone pattern in both the subject nouns and the subject pronouns. The declarative sentences will be rendered in the interrogative form so as to observe the position of the tone in the two constructions.

Interrogative Sentences:

257	Ọ̀ sàlụ̀ áfẹ́lẹ́?	Did he/she wash plates?
258	Fà nọ̀ n'ụ́nọ̀?	Are they in the house?
259	Àdá ọ̀ zàlụ̀ ụ́nọ̀?	Did Ada sweep the house?
260	Úchè ọ̀ sụ̀lụ̀ ákwà?	Did Uche wash clothes?
261	Íbè ò tòlù ógónógó?	Is Ibe tall?

Table 4-XLIX Tone in interrogative sentence constructions

From the foregoing, it is observed that the sentences can be discussed in two groups: First, it is observed that sentences (257) and (258) have subject pronouns and their interrogative form is formed by simply replacing the high tone of the pronouns Ọ and Fa with a low tone. The tones on the other elements of the constructions are constant. In sentences (259-261) which contain subject nouns, a resumptive pronoun ọ or o is introduced in each case. It is the resumptive pronoun that carries the low tone of interrogation in the sentences. The tones on the other elements remain constant in each case. The above is the usual method of forming interrogation in Ọnịcha and indeed in Igbo language in general. In the same way, when the other Igbo pronouns are used in such constructions above, the same process applies (i.e. replacement of high tones with low tones). For instance, únù *you (pl.)* becomes ùnù *you (pl.)* in interrogation. Ànyí *we* becomes ànyì; í *you (sing.)* becomes ì. Note that the low tone on the resumptive pronoun is the only phonological difference between the declarative and the interrogative sentences, which are otherwise structurally identical compare 252-256 with 257-261).

4.5.2 Functions of Tone in Derivation

In regular Ọnịcha Igbo usage, it is very common to see syntactic structures or sentences that are contracted in articulation/pronunciation and used as a single word. Emenanjo (1978:218) calls this derivational tonal morpheme, which he describes as being the same thing as tone patterns. He remarks that the derivational tonal morphemes can be used for deriving nouns from other structures, especially from sentences. It is observed that many of the Igbo names today are contractions of sentences. Some of these names are so deformed that it is sometimes quite difficult, if not impossible, to relate the distorted form to their original structures. Emenanjo gives some examples of sentences and the nominals that are derived from them. The following are some of his examples:

	SENTENCES		DERIVED NOMINALS
262a	Ọ dì ḿ'má H L H'H It is well/It is fine	262b	Ọ̀dìḿ'má LLH'H Welfare
263a	Ọ gà n'í'rú H L H'H He/she progressed	263b.	Ọ̀gàníí'rú LLHH'H Progress
264a	Á nù m̀ dí H L L H I got married	264b	Ànúḿdí LHHH Marriage
265a	Ó jì úkwú èjé H L HH LH He goes on foot	265b	Òjìúkwúèjé LLHHLH Pedestrian
266a	Ó jì é'gó àchọ́ é'gó H L H'H LH H'H He uses money to search for money	266b	Òjìé'góàchọ́é'gó LLH'HLHH'H Contractor

Table 4-L Nominals derived from sentences

From the foregoing examples, it is observed that the first or initial vowel which bears a high tone in the sentence form has a low tone in the derived nominal. The low tone here is not performing an interrogative function. It is rather performing a derivative (agentive) function. This implies that the lexicalization of sentences in Igbo follows the same process as in the grammatical functions of tones. Following Emenanjo's examples of nominals derived from sentences in Igbo by mere tone modification, we shall also examine other derivations from sentences in Ọnịcha Igbo. In this case, however, they may or may not include tone modifications.

The following are some examples of the personal names resulting from abridged structures:

	SENTENCES		DERIVED NOMINALS/NAMES
267a	Ífẹ́ á nà àchọ́ thing imp. aux. pref-*vb* pron. progr. *wish* What one is looking for	267b	Àchọ́
268a	Ẹ́*kwẹ́* à dị́ *n'* ìgwè pref-*vb* imp. vb *prep* N *agree* pron be *in* multitude Consent lies in unity	268b	Ẹ́kwẹ́dìgwè
269a	Ńdù kà ụ̀bá Life be wealth greater Life is greater than wealth	269b	Kúbà
270a	Nwá kà é'gó Child be money greater A child is greater than money		Nwaakaego/E'go/Nwaka
271a	Ọ̀nyẹ́ mà uche Chukwu? person know mind God Who knows the mind of God?	271b	Amauche/Amauchechu-kwu/Amauchechi
272a	Ọ̀nyẹ́ dị̀ kà Chúkwú? person be like God Who is like God?	272b	Ọnyẹka/Ọnyẹkachukwu/Ọnyẹkachi/Kachi

	SENTENCES		DERIVED NOMINALS/NAMES
273a	Nwá bù ùgwù Child be prestige A child is prestige	273b	Nwabuugwu

Table 4-LI Derivation of names from sentences

The above examples are Igbo names which have been derived from sentences; they may not have involved any modification in tones. They simply show that sentences could be lexicalized to derive Igbo names. The names in Ọnịcha Igbo could be said to be derived from the grammatical structures of the dialect. The list of the examples can be multiplied. The lexicalized names can be abridged or lengthened, as can be observed in the examples. The low tone on the pronoun above is not performing an interrogative function.

4.6 Summary of Derivational Affixes in the Ọnịcha Dialect of Igbo

		PREFIXATION				
			PREFIX	VR	SUFFIX	DERIVATIVE
1a	I	Infinitive	í=/ị́=	CV	-	í=/ị́= (CV)
	Ii	Perfect infinitive	í=/ị́=	CV	=go	í=/ị́=(CV)go
	Iii	Participle	a=/e=/ẹ=	CV	-	a=/e=/ẹ=
		PREFIXATION AND REDUPLICATION (SIMPLE GERUND/VERBAL NOUN)				
1b			PREFIX	VR	RdVR	DERIVATIVE
	I		ò=/ọ̀=	CV	CV_1-CV_2	ÒCV$_1$CV$_2$
		PREFIXATION AND SUFFIXATION				
			PREFIX	VR	SUFFIX	DERIVATIVE
1c	I	Group A	V	CV	-LV	V(CV)LV
	Ii	Group B	V	CV	C of VR & V of VR	V(CV)CV
	Iii	Group C	V	CV	ext of V of VR	V(CV)V

Table 4-LII Summary of derivation through prefixation

		INTERFIXATION					
2	A	NOUN-BASE FORM		N-I-N			
	B	VERB-BASE FORM	VP	VR	I	VP	VR
		i	V	CV	M	V	CV
		ii	V	CV	L	V	CV

Table 4-LIII Summary of derivation through interfixation

		DEVERBATIVES			
3	A	BCN			
			PREFIX	VR	DERIVATIVE
			à=/è=/ẹ=	CV	à=/è=/ẹ= (CV)
	B	GERUND (COMPLEX GERUNDS)			
			PREFIX	COMPLEX VERB	DERIVATIVE
			HHSN	CV_1CV_2	$HHSN(CV_1CV_2)$
	C	AGENTIVE			
			PREFIX	VR	DERIVATIVE
			ò=/ọ=	CV	ò=/ọ= (CV) + Noun complement
	D	NOUN INSTRUMENT			
			PREFIX	VR	DERIVATIVE
			LHSN	CV	LHSN (CV) + Noun complement
	E	NOUN OF RESULT			
			PREFIX	VR	DERIVATIVE
			LHSN	CV	LHSN (CV)
	F	MISCELLANEOUS DEVERBATIVES			
			PREFIX	VR	DERIVATIVE
		I	a=	CV	a(CV)
		Ii	e=	CV	e(CV)
		Iii	i=	CV	i(CV)
		Iv	o=	CV	o(CV)
		V	ọ=	CV	ọ(CV)
		Vi	ụ=	CV	ụ(CV)
		Vii	u=	CV	u(CV)
		Viii	m=	CV	m(CV)
		Ix	n=	CV	n(CV)

Table 4-LIV Summary of derivation through deverbatives

Chapter 5

Morpho-syntactic Features of Extensional Suffixes

5. Introduction

This chapter examines the morpho-syntactic analysis of extensional affixes in the Ọnịcha Igbo variety. Several extensional affixes are attested in the dialect. These affixes (suffixes) extend the meaning of the root or the base to which they are attached. The chapter examines the extensional suffix and the verb root so as to differentiate one from the other. It also attempts distinguishing extensional suffixes and enclitics; finally, it provides an analysis of extensional suffixes in the dialect.

The extensional suffixes are here classified into eight functional groups within which are a number of subclasses which are referred to as *extenders*. The functional groups are as follows:

5.1 Imperativeness, which includes the following extenders:
- inchoactive
- terminative

5.2 Temporality, which includes:
- anteriority
- frequentative
- durative

5.3 Direction, which includes
- motive
- dative
- locative
- benefactive

5.4 Contact, which includes
- fellowship
- fixative
- touch

5.5 Evaluation, which includes
- comparative
- partial
- relief

5.6 Reflexives, which include
- revisory
- retaliative

5.7 Termination, which includes
- completive
- conclusive

5.8 Miscellaneous, which include
- causative
- primal
- dispositional

Each of these extenders is explained with ample examples. The co-occurrence possibilities of the extensional suffixes are thereafter discussed; finally, the order of extensional suffixes is established.

Several analysts in Igbo studies have made different references to this class of suffixes, some, example Ndimele (2003:36) call it verbal extension, some, for instance Emenanjo (1975:89) call it lexical suffixes, Emenanjo (1978:97) call it meaning modifying suffixes. The morpho-syntactic analysis of extensional suffixes in Ọnịcha Igbo shall be examined under the following headings:

- Features of the extensional suffixes in Ọnịcha Igbo.
- Extensional suffix and verb roots
- Extensional suffix and Enclitics
- Analysis of extensional suffixes in Ọnịcha
- Co-occurrence possibilities of extensional suffixes
- Order of extensional suffixes
- Order of extensional and inflectional suffixes in a verbal sentence form.

5.1 Features of Extensional suffix
The features of extensional suffix in Ọnịcha Igbo are discussed under such topics as tone, syllable and vowel harmony of the extensional suffix. Syllable and vowel harmony had been discussed in chapter one of this book. Tone was also discussed in the previous chapter (chapter 4).

5.2 Extensional Suffix and Verb Root
The objective of this section is to distinguish the simple verb root from the affixes (derivational, extensional, and inflectional affixes). Many linguists have expressed their views on this. For instance, Katamba (1993:133) states that *morpheme ordering reflects the hierarchical ordering of strata*. He says that derivational affixes are nearer to the verb root than inflectional ones. Spencer (1991:193) and D Eka (2004:66), in their individual claims, assert that inflectional affixes are attached more peripherally to the stem than are the derivational ones. According to Spencer, the attachment of inflectional affixes external to the derivational ones is logical because the lexeme has to be derived by derivational processes first, before a set of inflectional forms of it can result. From the above discussions of the positions of verb root, derivational and inflectional affixes, it is observed that since the derivational affix is closer to the root, and the inflectional affix always on the periphery, the extensional suffix must be next and closer to the derivational ones whose meaning it extends from its definition.

In making these distinctions, the present research will use the model proposed by Emenanjo (1978:99). He defines an extensional suffix as a term used in African linguistics to refer to elements, usually affixes, which function principally as meaning modifiers. He defines inflectional affixes as suffixes which function with the inflectional verbal vowel prefix, auxiliaries, and syntactic tone patterns to mark the different aspects and verb forms in Igbo. Emenanjo (1978:99) defines verb root in terms of its cognate nature and states that: "An element is regarded as fully cognate with a verb when its morphological structure, inherent basic tone and meaning are identical with those of the basic form of a particular verb".

The cognate feature of a verb implies, therefore, that such a verb has a morphological, semantic, and tonal resemblance with the basic form of a known verb. Verb roots can generate elements, while extensional and inflectional suffixes cannot, but they can co-occur with cognate verbal elements in a construction. In our distinction of verb root from suffix, we shall consider morphemes that can occur independently as a monosyllabic verb base, as well as those that have morphological, semantic, and tonal resemblance with the basic form of a known verb. The following examples are illustrative:

7	Àdá	gòtèlù		éwú
	Ada	vb-*ext.suff.*-infl.suff.		goat
		buy		
	Ada bought a goat.			
8	Àdá	gònyèlù	ànyì	éwú
	Ada	vb-*v.element*-infl.suff.	us	goat
		buy *give*		
	Ada bought us a goat (≈ Ada bought a goat and gave us).			
9	Íbè	lìlì	énú	ósísí
	Ibe	vb-*infl.suff.*	up	tree
		climb		
	Ibe climbed up a tree.			
10	Íbè	lìbàlù	énú	ósísí
	Ibe	vb-*ext.suff.*-infl.suff.	up	tree
		climb		
	Ibe started climbing a tree.			

Table 5-I Distinction of verb root from extensional suffix

Considering the above examples, it is observed that examples (7) and (10) have extensional suffixes, while examples (8) and (9) do not contain extensional suffixes. How are we sure? What are the bases of the distinction? In analyzing the above, we shall consider the morphological, syntactic and semantic aspects of the verbal elements in the constructions. For instance, in sentence (7), the verbal element gòtèlù contains the following:

a. **-go** *buy* has a cognate element **ègó** *buying*. The inherent basic tone and meaning of the cognate element **ègó** is identical to the verb **-go**.
b. **=te** in the context of the above is an extensional suffix because it does not have a cognate element and its tone and meaning have no relation to the verb root. **=te** marks the direction to which the goat belongs. *Ada bought the goat for herself* and perhaps others.
c. **=lu** in the above verbal element is an inflectional suffix which marks a past action. The action of buying the goat is completed by the suffixation of the suffix **=lu**.

In sentence (10), the verbal element **lìbàlù** can be analysed as follows:
-lí *climb* has a cognate element **àlí** *climbing*. The inherent basic tone and meaning of the cognate element **àlí** is identical to the verb **-lí**. **=ba** is an extensional suffix that marks inceptive. It does not have a cognate element and its inherent basic tone and meaning are not identical to any verb.

Sentences (8) and (9) have no extensional suffix. The verbal element in (8) can be analysed as follows:

a. **-gó** *buy* is a known verb, it has cognate element **ègó**, *buying* can have meaning in isolation which is '*buy, buying*.
b. **-nyé** *give* is a known verb, has a cognate element **ènyé** *giving*, can have meaning in isolation. The inherent basic tone and meaning of the cognate element **ènyé** is identical to the verb **-nyé**.
c. **=lù** is an inflectional indicative suffix which marks the past action in the sentence. The action of buying was completed by the presence of the inflectional suffix in the sentence.

Sentence (9) has no extensional suffix. The verbal element **–lí** *climb*, as in sentence (10) is a known verb and the suffix **=lì** is an inflectional suffix which marks the past action in the sentence. Following Emenanjo's model, suffixes (extensional and inflectional) can be differentiated from verbs through the consideration of their morphological structure (whether or not a cognate element can be formed), and semantic structure (whether or not they have meaning in isolation and in environment).

5.3 Extensional Suffixes and Enclitics
The distinction needs to be made between extensional suffixes and enclitics because the two are identical in Igbo. A clitic is defined by Crystal (1997:64) as a form which resembles a word, but which cannot stand on its own as a normal utterance, being structurally dependent upon a neighbouring word in a construction. Clitics are of two types:

- Proclitics – those that depend upon a following word
- Enclitics – those that depend upon a preceding word

In Igbo, suffixes and enclitics occur so consistently and so prominently in constructions that Emenanjo (1978:90) recommends that they be raised to a part of speech. Both suffixes and enclitics are bound morphemes and they have identical syllabic structures. The two can, however, be distinguished in constructions. Suffixes are attached only to verbs while enclitics can attach to verbals and nominals alike.

In Ọnịcha, enclitics are attached to both verbals and nominals. They are written together with verbs when attached to verbals, but separately from non-verbals. Suffixes are always written together with verbs. Enclitics may or may not take the same tone patterns, as those of the preceding syllables. The following are some examples of enclitics in Ọnịcha:

- cha: *all; totality*
- dụ: *optional interrogative marker*
- ga: *optional plural marker*
- kwa: *also*; *in addition to* denoting repetition or emphasis
- kwu: *also; in addition to something else*
- nụ: *indicates politeness or mild request; please*
- nụ: *optional polite plural marker*
- nwa/nwà: *emphatic pronominal/nominal phrase marker very self*
- zi/zị: *after; afterward; now after some event else*

5.4 An Analysis of the Extensional Suffixes

This section examines the co-occurrence of verbs and extensional suffixes and their semantic characteristics in Ọnịcha Igbo constructions. Emenanjo (1978: 100-123) has an impressive list of extensional suffixes drawn from several dialects of Igbo. For the purposes of this book, however, a different approach into the extensional suffix *landscape* encountered in Ọnịcha Igbo is required. In addition, there is a need for these suffixes to be classed into groups that can easily be described and analyzed within the context of general linguistics. Therefore, in what follows, we classify the extensional suffixes according to their semantic and syntactic behaviour. And though we lay no claim to exhaustivity, we provide a catalogue of those extensional suffixes that are most frequently attested in synchronic usage. Some of these suffixes have appeared in studies conducted by earlier Igbo linguists, but others have so far not been mentioned in any literature, to the best of our knowledge. However, the classification of these suffixes is, as has been earlier noted, purely novel.

In what follows, we classify extensional suffixes semantically and syntactically into eight functional classes. Within each class are a number of subclasses which we refer to as ***extenders***. Extenders here refer to extensional suffixes which are used to realize the various semantico-syntactic functions examined below:

5.4.1 Imperativeness

Under the imperative function of extensional suffixes, we have the following extenders:

- Inchoactive Extenders
- Terminative Extenders

We have used the term imperative function, not because the extenders perform only imperative functions, but to highlight the contrastive functions that they can also perform. For instance, the inchoactive extender =ba/=be/=bẹ demonstrate inception of action as in:

11. lìbé - *start eating*
12. zàbá - *start sweeping*
13. jẹ̀bẹ́ - *start going*

The terminative extender =dẹ́bẹ́ demonstrates discontinuation of action already in progress as in:

14. lìdẹ́bẹ́ - *stop eating*
15. zàdẹ́bẹ́ - *stop sweeping*
16. jẹ̀dẹ́bẹ́ - *stop going*

The inchoactive extender has three forms =ba/=be/=bẹ which correspond to non-expanded and expanded vowel verb roots. It obeys the vowel harmony. Hence the suffix =ba/=bẹ co-occur with non-expanded vowels while =be co-occurs with expanded vowels. In Central Igbo and most other Igbo varieties, the inchoative extender is realized as =wa/=we and its syllabic structure is CV. Sometimes an inceptive morpheme 'ngwa' 'alright' (which cannot be adequately glossed because it has no one to one translation) is attached at the beginning to show that the action is actually at the inceptive stage. This, however, is not obligatory but it is realized occasionally in utterance. It is common in Ọnịcha to hear such expressions as:

17. Ń'gwá zàbá ụ́nọ̀ *Now/alright start sweeping the house*
18. Ń'gwá kwùbé *Now/alright start speaking*
19. Ń'gwá pùbá *Now/alright start going*

Note that ń'gwá is not actually translated as *now* or *alright* as we have glossed above. It is simply the nearest meaning or expression that can be found in English.

With respect to tone, the inceptive suffix =ba/=be maintains a high tone in all the constructions. The verb roots are all with low tone because they are imperative sentences where typically the verb roots are all reduced to low tone followed by open vowel suffix on a high tone. The terminative extender, on the other hand demonstrates the discontinuation of an action already started, as has been illustrated above. The terminative extender has only one form =dẹ́bẹ́, which co-occurs with both expanded and non-expanded vowels. It is invariable, and its syllabic structure is CVCV.

Affixation and Auxiliaries in Igbo 101

5.4.2 Temporality
Under temporality extensional suffixes in the Ọnịcha dialect of Igbo we have the following extenders:

- Anteriority Extenders =bu, which demonstrate temporal relations.
- Frequentative Extenders =gide/=dide, which demonstrate persistence.
- Durative Extenders =lịlị, which demonstrate doggedness.

5.4.2.1 Anteriority Extender
The anteriority extender =bu in the Ọnịcha variety of Igbo has one form which co-occurs with both expanded and non-expanded vowels. Its syllabic structure is CV. It copies the tone of the verb root to which it is attached. From the point of view of vowel harmony, the anteriority extender =bu is invariable. It co-occurs with both active and stative verbs. The following are examples of the co-occurrence possibilities of the anteriority extender in Ọnịcha.

20	Chí'ké bụ̀*bù* ónyé ńkúzí. Chike vb-*ant.extndr*.person teach be Chike was formerly a teacher/Chike used to be a teacher
21	Úchè nọ̀*bù* ẹ́bẹ́ à. Uche vb-*ant.extndr*. place this stay Uche was formerly here.
22	Ńnà yá *nà-àzụ́bú* á'fíá. Father him *aux.prog*-pref-vb-*ant.extndr*. market trade His/her father used to be a trader.
23	Fá lù*bù*lù ọ́lụ́ óyìbó. They vb-*ant.extndr*-infl.suff. work government work They used to be civil servants
24	Obi nwẹ̀*bù*lù é'gó. Obi vb-*ant.extndr*-infl.suff. money have Obi was formerly rich/Obi used to be wealthy.

Table 5-II Co-occurrence of anteriority extenders with verb roots

From the semantic point of view, the extender =bu denotes anteriority. It functions as a temporal adverbial which expresses an anterior situation of the action expressed by the verb. With active verbs, the anteriority extender =bu, denotes a habitual action in the past which has perhaps, ceased at the present time. When the extender =bu co-occurs with stative verbs, it expresses the former state of affairs of the patient.

5.4.2.2 Frequentative Extenders

The frequentative extender =dide/=gide in the Ọnịcha dialect of Igbo has one form which co-occurs with both the expanded and non-expanded vowels. =dide/=gide are in free variation, and can be used interchangeably. From the tonal point of view, the extender copies the tone of the verb root to which it is attached if there is no auxiliary preceding its verb, but if preceded by an auxiliary verb, the frequentative extender takes a high tone, as seen in the following examples:

25	Ànyí jè*dìdèlù* We vb-*freq.extndr*-infl.suff. go We walked till we were exhausted.	ìjè walk	'íké strength	gwụ́ finish	'ányí. we (object)
26	Àdáọ̀rà gù*dìdèlù* Adaora vb-*freq.extndr*-infl.suff. read Adaora read till daybreak.		ákwụ́kwọ́ book	chì day	fó. vb dawn
27	Únù gà-ánọ̀dídé You(pl.) *aux*-pref-*vb*-freq.extndr. modal stay You will stay here till evening.	ẹ́bẹ́ à place this		lúé reach	ḿgbèdè evening
28	Áfíá à nà-àzụ́dídé Market this *aux*-pref-*vb*-freq.extndr. prog. buy This market is open till nightfall.		chí day	'éjíé. blacken	
29	Ó rùbègìdèlù He/she vb-*freq.extndr*-infl.suff. bend He obeyed till death.		ísí head	lúé till	n'ọ́nwụ. *prep*-death

Table 5-III Co-occurrence of frequentative extenders with verb roots

With respect to the semantic interpretation, the frequentative extender =dide/=gide denotes persistence. The meaning of the construction containing the extensional suffix =dide/=gide is influenced by the preceding auxiliary, if any. With the presence of the modal auxiliary *ga*, the construction sounds like an instruction or a command as in example (27) above but with the auxiliary *na*, the construction denotes persistence or continuous action as in example (28).

5.4.2.3 Durative Extenders

The durative extender =lili/=lịlị in Ọnịcha Igbo has two forms which co-occur with expanded and non-expanded vowels. The two forms harmonize with the vowel of the verb roots. The syllabic structure of the durative extender is CVCV and it co-occurs with both active and stative verbs. The extender maintains a low tone when it is used in the indicative and is not preceded by any auxiliary, but when it is preceded by an auxiliary verb (whether primary or modal), =lili/=lịlị maintains a high tone as in the following examples:

30	Ọ́rjì	nọ̀*lịlị*		n'	ìló	
	Orji	vb-*dur.extndr.*		*prep.*	outside	
		stay		*in*		
	Orji is still outside.					
31	Ńná	'Ụ́jụ́	*nà-ákọ̀lịlị*			ú'gbó
	Father Uju		aux.prog-pref-*vb*-dur.extndr.			farm
			farm			
	Uju's father still farms.					
32	Àdá	gà-è*kwúlịlị*				éz͟ió'kwú
	Ada	*aux.mod*-pref-*vb*-dur.extndr.				truth
		speak				
	Ada will speak the truth.					
33	Úchè	bì*lịlị*		bẹ̀	ń'nẹ́	'yá
	Uche	vb-*dur.extndr.*		home	mother	pron
		live				him/her
	Uche still lives in her mother's house.					

Table 5-IV Co-occurrence of durative extenders with verb roots

Semantically, the durative extender =lili/=lịlị denotes persistence, continuity, or obligation. The exact denotation depends on the auxiliary verb that precedes the verb. For instance, if the durative extender =lili/=lịlị is attached to the verb without the presence of the auxiliary verb as in examples (30) and (33), it denotes continuity or persistence. The same meaning is expressed if it is attached to the verb preceded by the progressive auxiliary verb –na as in example (31). But if the durative extender =lili/=lịlị is attached to the verb preceded by the modal auxiliary verb –ga as in example (32), it denotes obligation. In the Central and other Igbo dialects, this extender is realized as =rịrị.

5.4.3 Direction
Under direction, we have the following extenders:

- Motive Extender =go which demonstrates motion upwards.
- Dative Extenders =ta/=te which demonstrate action towards communication partners.
- Locative Extenders =dẹ̀bẹ́ which demonstrate proximity.
- Benefactive Extenders =lụ which demonstrate applicative action.

5.4.3.1 Motive Extenders
The motive extender =go in Ọnịcha Igbo has only one form which co-occurs with both expanded and non-expanded vowels. It is invariable to vowel harmony and its syllabic structure is CV. The following examples explicate the co-occurrence of the motive extender with verb roots.

34	Àdá	nà-èbúgó		m̄'mílí	n'é'nú.	
	Ada	aux-pref-*vb*-mot.extndr prog *carry*		water	*prep*-up	
	Ada is carrying water upstairs.					
35	Úchè	tùgòlù	àkpà	yá	n'é'nú	ọ́chẹ́.
	Uche	vb-*mot.extndr.*-infl.suff *throw*	bag	her	*prep*-top	chair
	Uche threw up her bag to the chair.					
36	Íbè	gà-àlígó	énú	ósísí.		
	Ibe	aux pref-*vb*-mot.extndr. modal *climb*	high	tree		
	Ibe will climb up the tree.					
37	Ùnù	nà-ákwàgó		ụ́gbọ́	à n'úgwú?	
	You(pl)	aux-pref-*vb*-mot.extndr. prog *push*		vehicle	this *prep*-hill	
	Are you pushing this vehicle up the hill?					
38	Òbí	nègòlù	ányá	n'ụ́nọ̀.		
	Obi	vb-*mot.extndr.*-infl.suff. *look*	eyes	*prep*-house		
	Obi looked up to the house.					

Table 5-V Co-occurrence of motive extenders with verb roots

With respect to the semantic interpretations, the motive extender =go denotes height, upward movement. It performs adverbial function as evidence from the examples shows. If the extender is deleted in the examples, the meaning changes as seen in the following examples:

39	Úchè tùlù àkpà yá n'é'nú ọ́chẹ́	Uche threw her bag on the chair
40	Íbè gà-àlí énú ósísí	Ibe will climb a tree
41	Ùnù nà-ákwà ụ́gbọ́ à n'úgwú?	Are you pushing this car along the hill?
42	Òbí nèlù ányá n'ụ́nọ̀	Obi looked at the house/Obi looked after the house

Table 5-VI Constructions without the extender =go

Considering the above sentences without the extender =go, several modifications are observed. For instance, in example (39), the interpretation is that Uche threw her bag on the chair and perhaps picked it up again, as opposed to the example (35) which implies that the bag was thrown up and was probably left there. In example (41), the interpretation of the question is that the car is being pushed on the hill, i.e. that the car is on the hill and is being pushed along the hill rather than that the car is being pushed up the hill as in the question in example (37) above. All these subtle semantic nuances are associated with the presence of the extender.

5.4.3.2 The Dative Extenders

The dative extender =ta/-te in the Ọnịcha variety of Igbo has two forms which co-occur with expanded and non-expanded vowels. It harmonizes with the vowel of the verb root. Its syllabic structure is CV. The dative extender co-occurs mainly with active verbs and has a high tone in most constructions except where it co-occurs in an indicative construction, as in the following examples:

43	Bíkó bàtá n'únọ̀ Please vb-*dat.extndr.* *prep*-house enter in Please come into the house.		
44	Ò gótégó àchịchà? pron vb-*dat.extndr.*-perf.mark. bread He/she buy Has he/she bought bread?		
45	Fá nà-ápụ̀tá n'úgbọ́ànị pron aux.prog-pref-*vb*-dat.extndr. *prep*-car They go/exit in They are coming out from a car.		
46	Íké gà-èbúté ńní n'ùtútù Ike aux.mod-pref-*vb*-dat.extndr. food *prep*-morning carry in Ike will bring food in the morning.		
47	Ànyí chùtèlù mmí'lí n'ùmí pron vb-*dat.extndr.*-infl.suff. water *prep*-well We fetch in We fetched water from the well.		

Table 5-VII Co-occurrence of dative extenders with verb roots

Semantically, the dative extender denotes direction toward the speaker. What this means is that the action expressed by the verb is done with reference to the speaker because he/she is either involved in or will benefit from the action. For instance, in example (43), the verb –bà in isolation denotes *enter*, but with the extender =ta, its meaning is modified to read as *come in (toward the speaker)* meaning that the speaker is inviting someone to his direction. Similarly, in example (45), the verb -pù which denotes *go* in isolation becomes *come* when it co-occurs with the dative extender. This is because when the speaker uses -pù, he tells the interlocutor to go in a direction that is anywhere but toward the speaker. But if the dative extender =ta/=te is attached, the direction is automatically toward the speaker; the same verb root which was earlier translated as *go* will now be translated as *come* because the movement is toward the speaker. In some expressions that involve such verbs as bring; fetch; carry etc, the attachment of the dative extender to such verbs entails that whatever is brought, fetched, or carried etc is done for the welfare or benefit of the speaker. If, for instance, we have such expressions as:

48	Àdá	wètàlù		é'gó
	Ada	vb-*dat.extndr*-infl.suff		money
		take		
	Ada brought money.			
49	Ógè	gà-èbúté		ń'ní
	Oge	aux.mod-pref-*vb*-dat.extndr.		food
		carry		
	Oge will bring food.			

Table 5-VIII Dative extenders showing motion toward the speaker

It is observed from the above examples that the verbs wè *take* and bú *carry*, which ordinarily mean almost the opposite, are neutralized to mean *bring* because of the presence of the dative extender =ta/=te which shows that the items will be directed to the speaker. If, however, the speaker decides to direct that the items be taken in the opposite direction or away from himself/herself, the extender =ta/=te will be replaced by =ga to give the following:

50	Àdá	wègàlù	...	é'gó
	Ada	vb-*dat.extndr.*-infl.suff....		money
		take		
	Ada sent money to ...			
51	Ógè	gà-èbúgálù	...	ń'ní
	Oge	aux.mod-pref-*vb*-dat.extndr.-*infl.suff*....		food
		carry		
	Oge will carry food to ...			

Table 5-IX Dative extender showing motion away from the speaker

Note that in the last two examples, the verbs wè and bú maintain what they are glossed in isolation. In other words, they maintain their lexical meaning but will mean *away from the speaker* when ga is attached. Ga can, therefore, be seen as a deictic.

5.4.3.3 The Locative Extender

The locative extender =dèbé in Ọnịcha Igbo has one form which co-occurs with both expanded and non-expanded vowels. Its syllabic structure is CV-CV. The tone of the locative extender is low when used in the indicative construction, but when used in the imperative or with an auxiliary verb, it maintains its inherent tone, as illustrated in the examples below:

52	Ànyí	bídèbèlù		ụnọ̀	é'gó.
	We	vb-*loc.extndr.*-infl.suff.		house	money
		live			
	We live near the bank.				

53	Àdá	gà-ànọ́dèbẹ́		ń'nẹ́	'yá.		
	Ada	modal aux-*pref*-vb-*loc.extndr* stay		mother	her		
	Ada will stay near her mother.						
54	Únù	bíádèbèlù		ǹsó.			
	You(pl)	vb-*loc.extndr.*-infl.suff. come		near			
	You came near.						
55	Fá	kwụ́dèbèlù		ọ́nyẹ́	ńkúzí	'fá.	
	They	vb-*loc.extndr*-infl.suff. stand		person	teach	them	
	They stood near their teacher.						
56	Kpụ́dèbẹ́		ọ́'chẹ́	kà	í	nòdụ́	ànì.
	vb-*loc.extndr.* Draw		chair	comp.	pro you	vb-*encl* sit	down
	Draw near the chair and sit down.						

Table 5-X Co-occurrence of locative extenders with verb roots

With respect to the semantic interpretation, the extender =dèbẹ́ denotes proximity. It functions as an adverb which shows the distance from one object to another. When the extender =dèbẹ́ co-occurs with a verb preceded by the auxiliary verb *ga*, the construction gives an impression of an order or a command but when it co-occurs with the verb preceded by the auxiliary *na*, it indicates a progressive or a habitual action.

5.4.3.4 The Benefactive Extenders

The benefactive extender in Ọnịcha Igbo is =LV where V is any of the high back/non-back expanded or non-expanded vowels. The vowel of the suffix harmonizes with the vowel of the verb root. The syllabic structure of the benefactive extender is CV. The following examples are illustrative:

57	Ńnà	ḿ	kwààlù		m̀	àfẹ̀	ọ́fụ́ụ́
	Father pron		vb-*infl.suff*-ben.extndr. me sew		pron	dress	new me
	My father sewed a new dress for me/My father made me a new dress						
58	Fá	dèbèèlù			yà	ọ́nòdù	n'írú
	They	vb-*infl.suff*-ben.extndr. keep			pron him/her	seat in	*prep*-front
	They reserved a seat for him/her in front.						
59	Ọ́	gà-àkwụ́lụ́			ńwá	yá	ụ́gwọ́ ákwụ́kwọ́
	pron He/she	aux.mod-pref-*vb*-ben.extndr. *pay*			child	pron him/her	debt book
	He/she will pay his/her child's school fees.						

60	Àdá	sì*ì*lì		'yá	ńní
	Ada	vb-*infl.suff*-loc.extndr. cook		him/her	food
	Ada cooked for him/her.				
61	É'bó	chù*ù*lù	ńnẹ́	'yá	ḿmí'lí
	Ebo	vb-*infl.suff*-loc.extndr. fetch	mother	pron	water him/her
	Ebo fetched water for his mother.				

Table 5-XI Co-occurrence of benefactive extenders with verb roots

There is evidence of vowel lengthening in some of the examples above. This is due to the deletion of the consonant part of the suffix, leaving only the vowels which regressively assimilate all the features of the preceding vowel. The process is observed in examples (57), (58), (60) and (61). Refer to the section on inflectional affixes for more information on benefactive and inflectional affixes.

5.4.4 Contact Function
Under contact function of extensional suffixes, we have the following extenders:

- Fellowship Extender =kọ, which demonstrates associative relations.
- Fixative Extender =do, which demonstrates firmness of attachment to something.
- Touch Extenders =tụ, which demonstrates contact between bodies.

5.4.4.1 The Fellowship Extender
The fellowship extender =kọ in the Ọnịcha dialect of Igbo has one form which co-occurs with both expanded and non-expanded vowels. Its syllabic structure is CV and it is invariable from the point of view of vowel harmony. The following examples explicate the co-occurrence of the fellowship extenders:

62	Fá	bì*kọ*̀lù		*n*'òfú	ógbẹ̀
	They	vb-*fel.extndr.*-infl.suff. live		*prep*-one	street
	They lived together in one village/They lived in the same street.				
63	Íbè	nà	Òbí	nà-à*gụ́*kọ́	ákwụ́kwọ́
	Ibe	conj	Obi	aux-pref-*vb*-fel.extndr. prog *read*	book
	and/with				
	Ibe and Obi are schoolmates/Ibe and Obi are studymates.				
64	Ànyí	nà-è*sí*kọ́	ńní	nà	bẹ́ 'Ámáká
	We	aux-pref-*vb*-fel.extndr. prog *cook*	food	prep at/in	home Amaka
	We cook together in Amaka's house.				

Affixation and Auxiliaries in Igbo

65	Òbí	nà	Ézẹ̀	nọ̀*kọ̀*lù		*n'*ụ́nọ̀	úkà
	Obi	conj	Eze	vb-*fel.extndr.*-infl.suff. stay		*prep*-house	church
	Obi and Eze stayed together in the church.						
66	Ùnù		gà-á*kọ̀*kọ́		jí	ófú	ógè̀?
	You(pl)		aux-pref-*vb*-fel.extndr. modal *cultivate*		yam	one	time
	Will you plant yams together at the same time?						

Table 5-XII Co-occurrence of fellowship extenders with verb roots

The fellowship extender copies the tone of the verb root in the indicative constructions, as in (62) and (65) above. It also copies the tone of the verb root in other constructions, except in low tone verbs in constructions with auxiliary verbs, as in example (66). In such sentence constructions, the fellowship extender =kọ maintains a high tone, as in examples (63) and (66). In terms of vowel harmony, the fellowship extender =kọ is invariable.

With respect to its semantic interpretation, the extender =kọ denotes *togetherness*. It functions as an adverb of manner because it tells how the action expressed by the verb is carried out. It entails team work i.e. co-operating as a team in doing whatever action or notion is expressed by the verb. Apart from *working as a team*, the extender =kọ can also denote *working individually* but concurrently at the same time. For instance, in example (66), the planting of yam may not be done together as a team in the same farm, but rather, that the yams are planted in different places by different persons, but at the same period of time.

5.4.4.2 The Fixative Extender

The fixative extender =do in Ọnịcha has one form which co-occurs with both expanded and non-expanded vowels. The syllabic structure of the fixative extender is CV and it is invariable to vowel harmony, as observed in the following examples:

67	Ọ̀nyẹ́	kè*dò*lù	éwú	à?
	person	vb-*fix.extndr.*-infl.suff. tie	goat	this
	Who tied this goat?			
68	Àmáká	zọ̀*dò*lù	ákwụ́kwọ́	ụ́kwụ́
	Amaka	vb-*fix.extndr.*-infl.suff. press	book	leg
	Amaka pressed her leg against a book.			
69	Kù*dó*	ńtú	*n'*á̩já	
	vb-*fix.extndr.*	nail	*prep*-sand	
	Knock			
	Drive a nail into the wall.			

70	Fá ga̍-àgbádó ú̩kwú̩ n' ú̩zò̩
	They aux.-pref-*vb*-fix.extndr. leg prep door
	modal *run*
	They will press their legs against the door.

Table 5-XIII Co-occurrence of fixative extenders with verb roots

From the semantic point of view, the extender =do denotes *keeping a firm hold…; fast against…*; it functions as an adverb of manner describing how the action expressed by the verb is carried out. For instance, in the examples above, if the extender is deleted, the sentences will have different meanings from what they have. Let us take some examples: Deleting the extender from example (67) above, the sentence will read:

71. Ọnyẹ́ kè̩*lù̩*   éwú   à?
    person vb-*infl.suff.*   goat   this
           share
    Who shared this goat?/Who created this goat?

This sentence construction calls for two possible interpretations in the first instance:

- Who shared this goat? (either as animals or as meat)
- Who created this goat? (ambiguous)

It is only the extender =do in the example above, and in (67) in particular, that gives the idea of tying or fastening the goat to a stake. Similarly, the deletion of the extender =do in example (68) gives the following interpretation:

72. Àmáká   zò̩*lù̩*   ákwú̩kwó̩   ú̩kwú̩
    Amaka   vb-*infl.suff.*   book   leg
            step
    Amaka stepped on the book.

The idea of pressing her legs steadily on the book is absent because of the deletion of the extender. The same process applies to examples (69) and (70).

5.4.4.3 The Touch Extender

The touch extender =tụ in the Ọnị̀cha dialect of Igbo has one form and it has a narrow collocational range (it does not co-occur with many verbs). The touch extender expresses contact with either animate or inanimate objects, as in the following examples:

73	Àdâkù gà-ẹdẹ́tú̩ ḿmányá ó̩nú̩
	Adaku aux.mod-pref-*vb*-tch.extndr. wine mouth
	taste
	Adaku will taste the wine.

Affixation and Auxiliaries in Igbo

74	Ànyí	mètùlù		àfẹ̀	yá	áká
	We	vb-*tch.extndr.*-infl.suff. do		dress	pron him/her	hand
	We touched his/her dress.					
75	Áfẹ̀	Ùchè	nà-èmẹ́tú		ná	ḿmánụ́
	Dress	Uche	aux.prog-pref-*vb*-tch.extndr. do		prep in	oil
	Uche's dress is touching oil.					
76	Mètụ́		ń'wá áká	n'ísí		
	vb-*tch.extndr.* do		child hand	*prep*-head in		
	Touch the child on (his/her) head/Touch the child's head.					

Table 5-XIV Co-occurrence of touch extenders with verb roots

Semantically, the extender =tụ in the Ọnịcha Igbo dialect denotes contact – contact of person with person, or of person with object, etc. The contact can be with any part of the body but evidence from the examples shows that the verbs commonly used with the contact suffix are mẹ *do* and dẹ *taste*. When it co-occurs with the verb dẹ *taste*, the contact is normally with the tongue as in example (73). But when it co-occurs with the verb mẹ *do*, the contact may be with any part of the body.

In the Central Igbo dialect, the touch extender is sometimes used outside the context of contact. Most of the time, it is used in the variety to express a little, a bit of. For instance, the following utterances are common in the Central Igbo dialect.

77. chèrétụ́   *wait a bit*
78. nyètụ́ m   *give me small*
79. wèrétụ̣   *take small*

In the above constructions, the extender, rather than denote contact, expresses smallness, little quantity. It can also be attenuative. Here in the examples, the extender does not express contact, and this is typical of the Central Igbo dialect. In the Ọnịcha Igbo variety, similar expressions can be represented thus:

80. chẹ̀lụ́nụ́   *wait a bit*
81. nyẹ̀nụ́ m   *give me small*
82. wẹ̀lụ́nụ́   *take small*

One can say that the construction with =nụ in the Ọnịcha dialect of Igbo is attenuative. In other words, it is a highly modalized way of speaking. =nụ can, therefore, be used as a modalizer in such constructions.

5.4.5 Evaluation

Under evaluation, we have the following extenders:

- Comparative Extender =kalị which demonstrates evaluation of elements.
- Partial Extender =bili which demonstrates segments of a whole.
- Relief Extender =kwanyẹ which demonstrates partial assistance/aid.

5.4.5.1 The Comparative Extender

The comparative extender =kalị in Ọnịcha has one form which co-occurs with both expanded and non-expanded vowels. Its syllabic structure is CV-CV. It takes a low tone when it co-occurs with verbs in the indicative constructions, but when it co-occurs with verb roots preceded by an auxiliary, whether progressive or modal, it takes a high tone, as in the examples below:

83	Àdâkù tò*kàlịlị*	Úchè	ógónógó
	Adaku vb-*comp.extndr.*-infl.suff.	Uche	tallness
	grow tall		
	Adaku is taller than Uche.		
84	Íbè nà-è̩j*é̩kálí̩*	Òbí	ózí
	Ibe aux-pref-*vb*-comp.extndr.	Obi	errand/message
	prog *go*		
	Ibe is more disposed to run errands than Obi is/Ibe runs more errands than Obi does.		
85	Fà sì*kàlịlị*	É̩bó	ńní?
	They vb-*comp.extndr.*-infl.suff.	Ebo	food
	cook		
	Do they cook better than Ebo?		
86	Ọ́rjì gà-án*ọ̀kálí̩*	'Úbá	nwáyọ̀
	Orji aux-pref-*vb*-comp.extndr.	Uba	calm
	modal *stay*		
	Orji will be calmer than Uba.		

Table 5-XV Co-occurrence of comparative extenders with verb roots

With respect to its semantic interpretation, the extender =kalị denotes comparison. Igbo has morphological markings to distinguish between comparative and superlative. For instance, when two things/objects are compared, =kalị (comparative) is used but when more than two objects are compared (superlative), =kàlịsịlị is used, as in the following examples:

87	Úchè jò*kàlịlị*	Àdá	
	Uche vb-*comp.extndr.*-infl.suff.	Ada	
	be ugly		
	Uche is uglier than Ada (comparative).		

Affixation and Auxiliaries in Igbo 113

88	Úchè	jòkàlìsìlì	úmùǹ'nẹ́	'yá
	Uche	vb-*comp.extndr.*-infl.suff.	siblings	pron
		be ugly		him/her
	Uche is the ugliest of her brothers and sisters (→siblings)(superlative).			

Table 5-XVI Constructions with both comparative and superlative extenders

In sentences where (=kalị) the =lị is reduplicated, the =lị on the periphery is the inflectional suffix, but in the above examples, the inflectional suffixes are describing the state of being of the subjects, and therefore they express the present state of being of the agents.

5.4.5.2 The Partial Extender

The partial extender =bili in Ọnịcha has one form which co-occurs with both expanded and non-expanded vowels. Its syllabic structure is CVCV. Here are some examples of constructions with partial extenders:

89	Ùjú	gà-ẹ̀wẹ́*bìlí*	ú'gụ́	
	Uju	aux.fut-pref-vb-*par.extndr.*	vegetable	
		take		
	Uju will take some vegetables.			
90	Fá	kpó*bììlì*	gàrị́	
	They	vb-*par.extndr.*	garri	
		pack		
	They took some garri.			
91	Tá*bìlí*	á'nụ́		
	vb-*par.extndr.*	meat		
	chew			
	Eat/Chew some meat.			

Table 5-XVII Co-occurrence of partial extenders with verb roots

The extender has a narrow collocational range. It co-occurs with the verb *take* and its various forms. It is invariable and does not harmonize with vowels in construction.

5.4.5.3 The Relief Extender

The relief extender =kwanyẹ in Ọnịcha has one form which co-occurs with both expanded and non-expanded vowels as in the following examples:

92	Àdá	gà-àsụ́*kwànyẹ́lụ́*	'm̄	ákwà
	Ada	aux.fut-pref-vb-*rel.extndr.*-appl.	pron.	cloth
		wash		me
	Ada wil help me do the laundry.			

93	Bí'kó	tụ́tụ̀*kwànyẹ́lụ́*	'm̄	ákwụ́
	Please	vb-*rel.extndr.*-appl. pick	pron. me	palmnut
	Please help me pick palmnuts.			
94	Ànyị́	sí*kwànyẹ̀lụ́*	fá	ńní
	We	vb-*rel.extndr.*-appl. cook	pron. them	food
	We helped them in the cooking.			

Table 5-XVIII Co-occurrence of relief extenders with verb roots

The extender =kwanyẹ, as we observe in the sentences above, always co-occurs with the benefactive extender =lụ.

5.4.6 Reflexives
Under reflexives, we have the following extenders:

- Revisory Extenders =ghalị, which demonstrate reversal of action.
- Retaliative Extenders =kwụlụ, which demonstrate reprisal action

5.4.6.1 The Revisory Extender
The revisory extender =ghalị in the Ọnịcha dialect of Igbo has one form which co-occurs with expanded and non-expanded vowels. Its syllabic structure is CVCV. The tone of the revisory extender =ghalị is high when an auxiliary verb precedes the verb to which it is attached, but when it co-occurs with an inflectional suffix in an indicative construction, it maintains a low tone along with the verb root and the inflectional suffix. From the vowel harmony point of view, the extender =ghalị is invariable.

95	Úchè	sù*ghàlị̀lị̀*		ákwà	Àdá	sù*lụ̀*
	Uche	vb-*rev.extndr.*-infl.suff. wash		clothing	Ada	vb-*FT* wash
	Uche rewashed the clothing that Ada had washed.					
96	Òbí	gà-è*kwúghálí* *speak*		ífẹ́	ó	kwụ*lụ̀* speak
	Obi	aux-mod-pref-*vb*-rev.extndr.		thing	pron him/her	vb-*FT*
	Obi will repeat what he said/Obi will withdraw what he said.					
97	Íbè	nà-é*kòghálí* *hang*		ákwà	ńnà yá	kò*bèlù* him/her hang
	Ibe	aux-prog-pref-*vb*-rev.extndr.		clothing	father pron	vb-*FT*
	Ibe is transferring (elsewhere) the clothing hung by his father.					

Table 5-XIX Co-occurrence of revisory extenders with verb roots

The meaning of the constructions as denoted by the extender =ghalị is either redoing or withdrawing what was earlier said as in examples (95) and (96) respectively. In example (97), two interpretations are possible:

- Either that Ibe is transferring the clothing from the hanger in which his father had earlier hung it, or:
- Ibe is moving the clothing from one hanger to another.

In the Central Igbo variety, the extender =ghalị is realized as =gharị.

5.4.6.2 The Retaliative Extender

The retaliative extender =kwụlụ in the Ọnịcha variety of Igbo has one form which co-occurs with both expanded and non-expanded vowels. Its syllabic structure is CV-CV and it is invariable from the point of view of vowel harmony, as is seen in the following examples:

98	Òbí màlụ̀ Úchè ụ̀lá, Úchè má*kwụ́lụ́* 'yá Obi vb-*FT* Uche noun Uche vb-*ret.extndr*.pron. slap slap slap him/her Obi slapped Uche, Uche returned the slap.
99	Ọ́ zọ̀*lụ̀* m̀ úkwú, m̀ zọ̀*kwụ́lụ́* 'yá pron. vb-*FT* pron. leg pron. vb-*ret.extndr*.pron. He/she step me I step him/her He/she stepped on me, I stepped on him in return.
100	Fá tìlì yà ífẹ́, ò tí*kwụ́lụ́* 'fá pron. vb-*FT* pron. thing pron. vb-*ret.extndr*.pron. They beat him/her he/she beat them They beat him/her, he/she beta hem in return.
101	Àdá kwà*kwụ̀ụ̀lụ̀* Òbí áká ó̩ kwà*lụ̀* yá. Ada vb-*ret.extndr*.Obi hand pron. vb-*FT* pron. push he/she him/her Ada pushed Obi in retaliation.

Table 5-XX Co-occurrence of retaliative extenders with verb roots

In indicative constructions, the tone of the extender is low, thus harmonizing with the low tones of the verb root and the inflectional suffix, as in the following examples:

102	Òbí màkwụ̀ụ̀lụ̀ Úchè ụ̀lá	*Obi slapped Uche in return.*
103	Á zọ̀kwụ̀ụ̀lụ̀ m̀ yà úkwú	*I kicked him in return.*
104	Ó tìkwụ̀ụ̀lụ̀ fà 'ífẹ́	*He/she beat them in return.*

Table 5-XXI Retaliative extenders in indicative constructions

The above is the tonal behaviour of the retaliative extender in simple indicative constructions. With other constructions, the extender has a high tone, as in examples (98)-(100) above.

With respect to the semantic interpretation, the extender =kwụlụ denotes retaliation. This is mostly used in the Ọnịcha variety of Igbo. In the Central Igbo dialect, the extender mostly used is =gwara. The two extenders =kwụlụ (Ọnịcha) and gwara (Central Igbo) are sometimes interchangeably used by both Central Igbo and Ọnịcha Igbo dialect speakers. Both denote exactly the same thing.

5.4.7 Termination

Under termination, we have the following extenders:

- Completive Extenders =si/=sị, which demonstrate finality.
- Conclusive Extenders =tọpụ/=chapụ, which express termination of a stalled action.

5.4.7.1 The Completive Extenders

The completive extender =si/=sị in Ọnịcha has two forms which co-occur with both expanded and non-expanded vowels. Its syllabic structure is CV and it harmonizes with the vowel of the verb root, as seen in the following examples:

105	Àdá	lèsịlì	áfịá	'yá	nííné
	Ada	vb-*cpl.extndr*-infl.suff. sell	market	pron	all him/her
	Ada finished selling all her wares.				
106	Òbí	àgụ́sịgó	ákwụ́kwọ́		
	Obi	pref-*vb*-cpl.extndr.-*perf.mark* read	book		
	Obi has finished his studies.				
107	Ànyí	gà-èchúsí	m'mílí	ósí'só	
	We	aux.mod-pref-*vb*-cpl.extndr. fetch	water	quickly	
	We will finish fetching water quickly.				
108	Ụ́mụ̀	ákwụ́kwọ́ nà-èlísí	ńní	túpú	chí èjíé
	Children	book prog-pref-*vb*-cpl.extndr. eat	food	prep.	day darken
	School children finish their meal before nightfall.				
109	Dí'ké	ègwúsígó		'jí	'yá
	Dike	pref-*vb*-cpl.extndr-*perf.mark*. dig		yam	pron him/her
	Dike has finished harvesting his yams.				

Table 5-XXII Co-occurrence of completive extenders with verb

Semantically, the extender =si/=sị denotes *totality, finality,* or *completion* of a task. It shows that the action expressed by the verb is completely/totally realized by the agent. For instance, in the examples above, the presence of the extender is translated as *finish* in each of the examples. If the extender is deleted in example (105) for instance, the sentence will read:

Affixation and Auxiliaries in Igbo

110.   Ada sold her wares.

The idea that Ada exhausted the sales is therefore lost.

In the Central Igbo dialect, the same extender =si/=sị is represented by =cha or =kpọ so that the sentence will read:

111.   Àdá lèchàrà áhịá 'yá ní'ílé
112.   Àdá lèkpọ̀rọ̀ áhịá 'yá ní'ílé

Each of the above means exactly the same thing as example (105) above.

5.4.7.2 The Conclusive Extenders

The conclusive extender =tọ̀pù/=chàpù in Ọnịcha has one form which co-occurs with both expanded and non-expanded vowels. Its syllabic structure is CVCV and it is invariable to vowel harmony. The conclusive extender =tọ̀pù/=chàpù maintains a low tone in all the constructions, as in the examples which follow:

113	Ùjú gà-èlítọ̀pù Uju aux-pref-*vb*-ccl.extndr. *eat* Uju will finish eating this food.		ńní food	à this
114	Kwútọ̀pù vb-*ccl.extndr.* say Finish what you want to say (≈ Finish what you were saying).	ífé ị́ thing you wish	chọ̀lù vb-*FT*	í'kwú pref-*vb* *say*
115	Ànyị́ zátọ̀pụ̀lù We vb-*ccl.extndr*-infl.suff sweep We completed/finished up the compound sweeping.		èzí compound	
116	Òbí chọ̀lù Obi vb-*FT* wish/want Obi wants to complete/finish his work.	í'lútọ̀pù pref-*vb*-ccl.extndr. *work*	ọ́lú work	'yá his

Table 5-XXIII Co-occurrence of conclusive extenders with verb roots

=tọ̀pù can be used interchangeably with =chàpù in some contexts, in some other contexts, =chàpù can express a fresh action that is started and completed immediately but =tọ̀pù expresses the termination of a stalled action. =tọ̀pù/chàpù has been used here as conclusive extender; we are aware that pù in isolation is a verb, but it can be one of those verbs which has fossilized to an extender when in combination with tọ̀. =gbado can also be subsumed under the conclusive extenders. It is, however, different from the extender =tọpụ in the sense that it does not need to be concerned with a stalled action. =gbado can be applied to an action that has been started and completed;

the essential thing about it is that it entails entirety as shown in the following examples:

117	Òbí súgbàdòlù Obi vb-*ccl.extndr*-infl.suff wash Obi washed all the clothes.	ákwà cloth	ní'né all	
118	Ànyị gà-ègógbàdó We aux.fut-pref-vb-*ccl.extndr*. buy We will buy all these books.	ákwụ́kwọ́ book	ndị́ those	à this
119	Ézè chúgbàdòlù Eze vb-*ccl.extndr*-infl.suff dismiss Eze dismissed all his servants.	ụ́'mụ́ children	òdìbò servant	'yá his
120	Dẹ́gbàdó vb-*ccl.extndr*. iron Iron all these clothes.	ákwà cloth	ní'íné all	à this

Table 5-XXIV Co-occurrence of the extender =gbado with verb roots

It is observed from the foregoing examples that the extender =gbado has only one form which co-occurs with both expanded and non-expanded vowels. From the vowel harmony point of view, it is invariable. The extender =gbado co-occurs very frequently with *niine* all. In other words, *niine* can very easily follow the extender =gbado in all contexts because it also has the meaning *all*. The two extenders =tọpụ̀ and =gbado are very closely related and can be used interchangeably in some contexts. The subtle difference between the two is that while =tọpụ̀ in construction suggests finish up/complete what has already started, =gbado in construction does not imply such details. The action expressed by the verb is just considered in its entirety.

5.4.8 Miscellaneous

The following extenders, which cannot easily be grouped together logically are also attested in Ọnịcha:

- Causative Extenders =ba/=be, which demonstrate cause of action.
- Primal Extenders =godu, which demonstrate the first action in a sequence.
- Dispositional Extenders, in which the extenders are varied and express individual attitudes and idiosyncrasies.

    o =tọkọ   -   untidyness
    o =ghalị/=gheli   -   purposelessness
    o =zị   -   resignation

Affixation and Auxiliaries in Igbo 119

5.4.8.1 The Causative Extenders

The causative extender =ba/=be in Ọnịcha has two forms which co-occur with non-expanded and expanded vowels. Its syllabic structure is CV. The extender =ba co-occurs with all the non-expanded vowels while =be co-occurs with the expanded vowels. From the tonal point of view, the causative extender copies the tone of the verb root to which it is attached unlike that in the inceptive (with imperative sentences) which is consistently high. It co-occurs with both active and stative verbs, as shown in the examples below:

121	Fá kwù*bà*lù They vb-*cau.extndr*-infl.suff. stand They caused us to stand/They kept us standing. [→ kwú ọ́tọ́ *stand*]		ànyị us	ọ́tọ́ stand
122	Íbè tù*bà*lù Ibe vb-*cau.extndr*-infl.suff. throw Ibe caused Ada to become pregnant. [→ tú ímé *be pregnant*]		Àdá Ada	ímé inside
123	Ó yì*bè*lù He/she vb-*cau.extndr*-infl.suff. wear He/she caused the child to be dressed. [→ yí àfè *dress*]		nwátà child	àfè dress
124	Àdá bù*bè*lù Ada vb-*cau.extndr*-infl.suff. carry Ada caused her husband to starve. [→ bú ọ́nụ́ *starve*]	dí husband	yá her	ọ́nụ́ mouth
125	Ụ̀mù 'Óbí chì*bè*lù Children Obi vb-*cau.extndr.*-infl.suff. annoint Obi's children caused him to be crowned king. [→ chí ẹ̀zẹ̀ *crown king*]		yà him	ẹ̀zẹ̀ king

Table 5-XXV Co-occurrence of the causative extenders with verb roots

From the point of view of meaning, the causative extender =ba/=be functions as part of the verbal group. In other words, many of the verbs in the examples have inherent complements. The causative role of the extender =ba/=be is realized if and only if the verbal element containing the extender =ba/=be precedes a noun or a pronoun as evidenced in the examples above. Otherwise, the extender will function as an inchoative extender. Hence, if the objects (anyi, Ada, nwata, di, ya) in examples (121)-(125) above are deleted, the causative meaning will be lost and the sentences will have an inceptive interpretation as in the examples (126)-(130) below:

126	Fá kwùbàlù ótó	They started standing up
127*	Íbè tùbàlù í'mé	Ibe started bearing children/becoming pregnant
128	Àdá bùbèlù ó'nú	Ada started fasting
129	Úmù yá chìbèlù ézè	His children started taking titles
130	Ó yìbèlù àfè	He/she started dressing/wearing dress

Table 5-XXVI Constructions without objects resulting in inceptive interpretation

Note that sentence (127) is grammatical but unacceptable because the selectional restriction rule is violated. Ibe is masculine and therefore cannot be pregnant and bear children because pregnancy is + female. Ibe as male can only cause a female member to be pregnant. This modification in meaning is caused by the deletion of the object. The rest of the sentences are grammatical and acceptable but their semantic interpretations are different from what they are with the presence of the object.

5.4.8.2 The Primal Extender

The primal extender =godu in Ọnịcha has one form which co-occurs with both expanded and non-expanded vowels. Its syllabic structure is CVCV and it is invariable to vowel harmony. It copies the tones of the verb root, as observed in the following examples:

131	Bìágódú vb-pri.extndr. come Come first of all.	
132	Ànyí gà-èlígódú We aux-pref-*vb*-pri.extndr. modal *eat* We will first of all eat.	ń'ní food
133	Úzò làrùgòdùlù Uzo vb-*pri.extndr.*-infl.suff. sleep Uzo first of all slept.	úlá sleep
134	Fá gà-ènwégódú They aux-pref-*vb*-pri.extndr. modal *have* They will first of all exercise patience.	ǹdìdì patience
135	Á'gú nà-àsúgódú Agu aux-pref-*vb*-pri.extndr. prog. *wash* Agu is actually washing clothes.	ákwà cloth

Table 5-XXVII Co-occurrence of the primal extender with verb roots

With respect to semantic interpretation, the extender =godu denotes *first of all, at first*. It functions as an adverb. Its presence in a sentence indicates that the action expressed by the verb it is attached to must be performed first or rather must take priority over all other actions. For instance, in the examples, the intention expressed by each verb must be fulfilled first before any other thing.

5.4.8.3 The Dispositional Extenders

In this study, we take dispositional extenders to mean those extensional suffixes that demonstrate the inclination of an individual. We have recorded the following as dispositional extenders:

- =tòkọ́
- =ghalị/=gheli
- =zi

=tòkọ́ is one of the dispositional extenders. It is usually used to refer to actions or words/speech that are not edifying. As a matter of fact =tọkọ denotes untidiness. Its syllabic structure is CVCV. The following are some examples of expressions that contain such a dispositional extender =tọkọ:

| 136 | Gíní ká Òbí nà-àsítòkọ́ dụ́?
What foc Obi aux.prog-pref-vb-*disp.extndr.* encl.
  say
What nonsense is Obi saying? |

Table 5-XXVIII Co-occurrence of the dispositional extender with verb root sị

We note that there is an element of disgust in the speaker's question, which is more derisive than questioning.

| 137 | Fá nà-èrútòkọ́ ẹ́bẹ́ níné ḿmí'lí
They aux.prog-pref-vb-*disp.extndr.* place all water
  pour
They are pouring water all over the place (implied: thus making the whole place untidy). |
| 138 | É'bítòkòzịnà àfẹ̀ ḿ
Imp.pref-*vb*-disp.extndr-*disp.extndr*-neg.imp.morpheme dress me
  touch
Stop touching (≈ soiling) my dress. |

Table 5-XXIX Co-occurrence of the dispositional extenders with action verbs

It is observed from the above examples that the extensional sufiix =tọkọ denotes untidiness in whatever construction that it occurs. It has narrow colocational range because it cannot co-occur with many verbs.

=ghalị/=gheli is one of the dispositional extenders. It is used to refer to an uncoordinated or purposeless act in the context where =ghalị/=gheli are used. Its syllabic structure is CVCV. The following are examples of the extender in constructions:

139	Ụ̀mụ̀ ákwụ́kwọ́ nà-à*kwụ́*ghálị̀ *n*'ìló.
	Children book prog-pref-*vb*-disp.extndr. *prep.*-outside
	stand
	School children are perambulating outside.
140	Ùjú nà-à*chọ́*gháli̩ ọ'ché.
	Uju prog-pref-*vb*-disp.extndr. chair
	search
	Uju is anxiously looking for a seat.
141	Gị́'nị́ dụ́ kà Àdá nà-à*sí*ghèlí?
	What encl. foc Ada prog-pref-*vb*-disp.extndr.
	say
	What rubbish is Ada talking?

Table 5-XXX Co-occurrence of the dispositional extender =ghalị/=gheli with verb roots

The extenders in the above examples denote some *unchecked, random behaviour*. With the extender =ghalị, the construction describes the comportment of school children who *walk about aimlessly outside*. With the extender =gheli, the construction overtly shows recklessness on the part of the subject. =ghalị implies restlessness. =gheli implies foolishness.

=**zi** is one of the dispositional extenders. It is used to refer to the attitude of the subject *who willingly or unwillingly submits to the opinion of another*. Its syllabic structure is CV. The following are some examples of the co-occurrences of the dispositional extender =zi with verb roots:

142	Chúkwú mà*zì* ị́fẹ́ gá-ẹ̀mẹ̀'nú
	God vb-*disp.extndr.* thing aux.mod-pref-*vb*-encl.
	know *do/happen*
	God knows what will eventually happen.
143	Ọ̀nyẹ́ nà-è*sízí* ńní áfụ̀ ?
	Who aux.prog-pref-*vb*-disp.extndr. food that
	cook
	Who is eventually cooking that food?
144	Éwú 'ọ́nẹ́ kà fá gà-è*gbúzí* ?
	Goat how many foc. pron aux.mod-pref-*vb*-disp.extndr.
	they *kill*
	How many goats will they eventually kill?
145	Ńné nà Ńná 'Ádá bì*zì* *n*'ímé òbòdò
	Mother and Father Ada vb-*disp.extndr.* prep-inside country
	live in
	Ada's parents now live in the country.

Affixation and Auxiliaries in Igbo 123

146	Únù	màzì
	pron	vb-*disp.extndr.*
	You(pl)	know
	It is up to you (≈That's now your business, I'm no longer interested)	

Table 5-XXXI Co-occurrence of the extender =zi with verb roots

From the foregoing examples, it is observed that the dispositional extender =zi has one form which co-occurs with both expanded and non-expanded vowels. It copies the tone of the verb root to which it is attached.
From the vowel harmony point of view, the dispositional extender =zi harmonizes with the vowel of the verb root to which it is attached. It co-occurs with both active and stative verbs.

From the semantic point of view, the dispositional extender =zi denotes total abandonment to the will of God or to the opinion of the other member/members in the group. It expresses finality and the consent of the interlocutor to yield to the other person's suggestions. For instance, in example (146), there is total abandonment to the opinion of the únù *you (pl.)* which is the subject of sentence example (146). The locutor has apparently accepted willingly or unwillingly the decision of the interlocutor. In example (142), there is total surrender to the will of God. The means of expressing this *total surrender* or abandonment is associated with the presence of the extender =zi. In examples (143) and (144), the impression underlying their constructions may be that there had been arguments about who will do the cooking; about how many goats are to be slaughtered, etc. Perhaps a decision was taken in the end, and at a time when the speaker was not around. Such a situation could prompt the speaker to ask such questions as in the above. The interpretation of example (145) may be that Ada's parents, who were earlier living in the city, now live in the countryside. The dispositional extender =zi expresses, therefore, the resignation, total abandonment, and the last option left to the individual.

=zì has been grouped elsewhere in the literature as an enclitic. We totally agree with its status as an enclitic and we suggest in this work that, in addition to being an enclitic, it can also double as an extender whenever it is attached to a verb because of the function it performs in the construction. It can, however, pass for an enclitic when attached to nouns.

5.5 Co-occurrence Possibilities of Extensional Suffixes
This section discusses the combinability of extensional suffixes in Ọnịcha. The extensional suffixes in Ọnịcha Igbo, apart from co-occurring with verb roots, co-occur also with other extensional suffixes. This study intends to investigate the co-occurrence possibilities of the extensional suffixes in the Ọnịcha variety of Igbo. In investigating the co-occurrence possibilities of extensional suffixes, one important question to be considered is: *Does the co-occurrence of extensional suffixes take place arbitrarily, or is there an internal constraint that regulates or governs the combination of extensional suffixes, and, if there is a constraint, is it specifiable?*

Deriving the answers to these questions will involve combining different verbs with several extensional suffixes in order to determine the extent of the co-occurrence and the order of the extensional suffix with a given verb root.

On considering the co-occurrence possibilities of extensional suffixes in the Ọnịcha variety of Igbo, we shall be concerned with those extensional suffixes that have more frequent occurrence in combination. It is observed that as many as five extensional suffixes can co-occur in a single word as in kpòkọ́tábágódúlú... *begin first by gathering together for...*, where:

- kpò → verb root (gather/collect together)
- kọ́ → fellowship extender
- tá → dative extender
- bá → inchoative extender
- gódú → primal extender
- lú → benefactive extender

Notice that five extensional suffixes have co-occurred with a single verb root to yield one complete utterance. This is about the highest number of extensional suffixes that can co-occur in a word given the available data. Four, three, and two extensional suffixes can also co-occur in the dialect. An example of the co-occurrence of four extensional suffixes in a word can be attested by deleting the benefactive extender =lu/=lụ of the above example. For the co-occurrence of three extensional suffixes in a word, the infinitive form of the verb will be used in the operation for pedagogical and systematic reasons. We shall start with the dative extender =ta/=te. This co-occurs with the verb root -pù *go out* in the following order:

- Verb root → pù *go out*
- Infinitive → ịpù *to go out*
- Verb root + infinitive + dative extender → ịpụ̀tà *to come out*
- Verb root + infinitive + dative extender + inceptive → ịpụ̀tàbà *to start coming out*
- Verb root + infinitive + dative extender + inceptive + primal → ịpụ̀tàbàgòdù *to start coming out first*

These extensional suffixes have again co-occurred with a single verb root to yield one complete utterance. The semantic interpretation of the verb is radically modified as a result of the presence of the dative extender. For instance, the infinitive ịpù in isolation denotes *to go out*; with the dative extender =ta, the verb gives ịpụ̀tà *to come out* (motion toward the speaker).

From the above co-occurrence of the verb root with the three extensional suffixes, it is observed that a particular order is followed in their combination, and it is as follows:
Verb root + dative extender + inchoative extender + primal extender

If the above order is reversed for the construction, an ungrammatical and unacceptable utterance will result, as in:

- *ịpụ̀gòdùtàbà
- *ịpụ̀tàgòdùbà
- *ịpụ̀bàgòdùtà

The three utterances above are all ungrammatical because of the order or the (internal) arrangement of the suffixes. The acceptable utterance ịpụ̀tàbàgòdù contains exactly the same suffixes, and it is only the order that has rendered the three above ungrammatical. The extender =godu appears to be very productive for the fact that it can readily co-occur with most other extensional suffixes. In the combination, =godu always appears at the end (at the periphery), except when it is followed by the applicative extensional suffix, which always stays at the end, even with inflectional suffixes. It is observed that =godu can commute with frequentative (=dide/=gide) and durative (=lili/=lịlị) in the same position to give: ịpụ̀tàgìgdè *to keep coming out*, and ịpụ̀tàlịlị *to continue coming out*.

Note that ịpụ̀tàgìdè and ịpụ̀tàlịlị appear to mean the same as presented above. The difference between the two can be explained in context, with sentence constructions, as in the following examples:

147	Úchè	gà-è*chẹ́g*ídé	ẹ́bẹ́	à
	Uche	aux.mod-pref-*vb*-ext.suff. *wait*	place	this
	Uche must persistently wait here.			
148	Úchè	nà-è*chẹ́g*ídé	ẹ́bẹ́	à
	Uche	aux.prog-pref-*vb*-ext.suff. *wait*	place	this
	Uche waits here persistently.			
149	Àdá	gà-è*chẹ́l*ịlị́	ẹ́bẹ́	à
	Ada	aux.mod-pref-*vb*-ext.suff. *wait*	place	this
	Ada must persistently wait here.			
150	Àdá	nà-è*chẹ́l*ịlị́	ẹ́bẹ́	à
	Ada	aux.prog-pref-*vb*-ext.suff. *wait*	place	this
	Ada is still waiting here.			

Table5-XXXII Distinction between frequentative and durative extenders

The difference between the two extenders =gide/=dide and =lili/=lịlị is made clearer from the examples above. For instance, when =gide/=dide co-occurs with a modal auxiliary verb -*ga*, it connotes obligation and some degree of certainty. When it co-occurs with a progressive auxiliary, it connotes persistence and some element of perseverance. Again, when the extender =lili/=l̨il̨i co-occurs with the modal auxiliary verb –ga, it connotes obligation and compulsion, but when it co-occurs with the progressive auxiliary verb –na, it connotes persistence and perseverance. In other words, the interpretation of the two extensional suffixes depends on the context and the type of auxiliary verb that goes with them.

The verb root -pù *go out* which has been used in the process above can be substituted with another verb root –bà *enter* to get exactly the same structure as with -pù as follows:

- bà *enter*
- ịbà *to enter*
- ịbàtà *to enter toward*
- ịbàtàbà *to begin to enter toward*
- ịbàtàbàgòdù *to begin to enter toward, first of all*

=godu can again be substituted with =gide/=dide and =lili (after deleting the inceptive) to get the following:

- ịbàtàgìdè *to enter continuously/persistently*
- ịbàtàl̨il̨ì *to enter continuously/persistently*

Just as was done with the verb root -pù, the co-occurrence of the above with the auxiliary –ga (modal) and –na (progressive) will differentiate clearly the apparently subtle difference of ± obligation and persistence in the two complex words.

Many other combinations of verb roots and extensional suffixes can exist in the dialect, but, as was said at the beginning of the chapter, the work can only examine the most frequent ones in combination.

5.5.1 Order of Extensional Suffixes

The co-occurrence possibilities and order of different extensional suffixes can be summarized in a grid as presented below. The key to the grid is as follows:

    A. Fellowship extender =kọ (together)
    B. Dative extender =ta/=te (to/for)
    C. Inchoative extender =ba/=be (start/begin)
    D. Motive extender =go/=(da***) (motion upward/downward)
    E. Frequentative extender =dide/=gide (persistently)
    F. Locative extender =dẹbẹ (near)
    G. Completive extender =sị (finish)
    H. Durative extender =l̨il̨i (continuously ± obligation)
    I. Primal extender =godu (first/at first)
    J. Benefactive extender =lu/-lụ (for/on behalf of)

Affixation and Auxiliaries in Igbo

		Verb Root	Extenders									Indirect Object Pronoun/ Noun
		A	B		C	D	E	F	G	H	I	J	
1	zá *sweep* bú *carry* chọ́ *search*		kpó *gather*	kọ ta	Ba						godu	lu	m ya anyị fa Obi Ada ndị afụ
2	chú *fetch* zú *steal*		te		Be						godu	lụ	
3	bí *live* nọ̀ *stay* kpụ́ *shift*								dẹbẹ		godu		
4	tụ́ *throw*					go da	gide						
5	bú *carry*					go				lịlị			
6	bú *carry*					go					godu	lu	
7	bú *carry*		te					gide			godu	lu	
8	gọ́ *deny*						gide				godu		
9	bà *enter*		ta		Ba						godu		
10	gụ́ *read/count* kwụ̀ *pay*				Ba						godu	lu	
11	kwụ *pay* gụ *read*									sị	lịlị		
12	kwụ *pay* gụ *read*									sị		godu	lu	

Table 5-XXXIII Co-occurrence possibilities and order of extensional suffixes

From the above examples of the co-occurrence possibilities of extensional suffixes, it is observed that the disyllabic extensional suffixes co-occur more frequently/readily with the monosyllabic extensional suffixes and even with themselves. It is observed that the extender =godu has the highest frequency in distribution. It can co-occur with most extensional suffixes and, in combination, it is always found at the periphery except if it co-occurs with the benefactive extender =lu/=lụ. The benefactive extender is always the last suffix possible in a word.

Having seen the extenders that can co-occur, we shall, in what follows, examine those that cannot co-occur. For instance, the following extenders cannot co-occur:

Inchoactive =ba/=be/=bẹ cannot co-occur with Terminative =dẹbẹ
e.g. verb root =sí *cook*; extenders =ba/=be/=bẹ/=dẹbẹ
Hence *síbẹ́dẹ́bẹ́ is unacceptable

Inchoactive =ba/=be/=bẹ cannot co-occur with Conclusive =tòpù
e.g. verb root =kwú *speak*; extenders =ba/=be/=bẹ/=tòpù
Hence *kwúbetòpù is unacceptable

Frequentative =dide cannot co-occur with Terminative =dẹ́bẹ́
e.g. verb root =lí *eat*; extenders =dide/=dẹ́bẹ́
Hence *lídidedẹ́bẹ́ is unacceptable

Frequentative =dide cannot co-occur with Completive =si
e.g. verb root =lụ́ *work*; extenders =dide/=si
Hence *lụ́didesi is unacceptable

Terminative =dẹ́bẹ́ cannot co-occur with Conclusive =tòpù
e.g. verb root =sụ́ *wash*; extenders =dẹ́bẹ́/=tòpù
Hence *sụ́dẹ́bẹ́tòpù is unacceptable

Anteriority =bu cannot co-occur with Durative =lili/=lịlị
e.g. verb root =bù; *be* extenders =bu/=lili/=lịlị
Hence *bùbùlili is unacceptable

Motive =go/=da cannot co-occur with Fixative =do
e.g. verb root =bú *carry*; extenders =go/=da/=do
Hence *búgódó/búdàdó are unacceptable

Locative =dèbẹ́ cannot co-occur with Fixative =do
e.g. verb root =kwụ́ *stand*; extenders =dèbé/do
Hence *kwụ́dèbẹ́dó is unacceptable

Affixation and Auxiliaries in Igbo

Anteriority =bu cannot co-occur with Inchoactive =ba/=be/=bẹ
e.g. verb root =zà *sweep*; extenders =bu/=ba/=be/=bẹ
Hence *zàbúbá is unacceptable

Relief =kwànyẹ́ cannot co-occur with Motive =go/=da
e.g. verb root =gụ́ *count*; extenders =kwànyẹ́/=go/=da
Hence *gukwànyẹ́go or gukwànyẹ́da is unacceptable

The meaning expressed by the extender in a sentence depends on the presence or absence of some other elements in that construction. For instance, when the extender =lịlị (continuative) occurs in a sentence with a modal auxiliary verb -*ga* plus verb root, an obligation is implied in the meaning, as in:

> 151. Àdá   gà   à*nọ̀lị́lị́*   n'ụ́nọ̀
>   Ada   aux.   pref-*vb*-dur.extndr.   prep-house
>   will   *stay*
>   Ada must stay in the house.

If, on the other hand, the modal auxiliary is absent in the sentence that contains the extender =lịlị, the implication is continuity, as in:

> 152. Àdá   *nọ̀lịlì*   n'ụ́nọ̀
>   Ada   *vb*-dur.extndr.   prep.house
>   *stay*   in
>   Ada is still in the house.

The interpretation of example (151) is twofold.
- Ada must stay in the house.
- Ada may still be in the house.

It is the context of usage that will disambiguate the construction.

5.5.2 Order of Extensional and Inflectional Suffixes

Evidence from the examples we have seen all through this work shows that extensional and inflectional suffixes appear in particular positions in Ọnịcha and in all Igbo constructions. The order brings the extenders closer to the verb root than the inflectional suffixes. The following examples explicate further the ordering of the suffixes in Ọnịcha Igbo constructions:

153	Úchè wẹ̀*tà*lụ̀ é'gó
	Uche vb-*dat.extndr.*-infl.suff. money
	bring
	Uche brought money.

154	Ńnà	fá	lùbùlù		ólú	óyìbó
	Father	pron them	vb-*ant.extndr*.-infl.suff. work		work	government
	Their father formerly worked in the civil service/Their father was formerly a civil servant.					
155	Àdá	nòdìdèlù		n'ụ̀nọ̀	tátà	
	Ada	vb-*freq.extndr*.-infl.suff. stay		*prep*-house in	today	
	Ada stayed indoors today.					
156	Íbè	tùbàlù		Ńgọ́zí	ímé	
	Ibe	vb-*cau.extndr*.-infl.suff. impregnate		Ngozi	pregnant	
	Ibe impregnated Ngozi. [Note: tu…ímé ICV]					
157	Úchè	nà	Àdá	gùkọ̀lù	ákwụ́kwọ́	n'òfú	ẹ́'bẹ́
	Uche	conj. and	Ada	vb-*fel.extndr*-infl.suff. read	book	*prep*-one in	place
	Uche and Ada studied in the same place.						

Table 5-XXXIV Order of extensional and inflectional suffixes

Exceptions

Some constructions in the Ọnịcha Igbo variety do not, however, conform to the order as stated above. There are a few cases where the extender stays at the outer layer or the periphery of the verbal group, as in the following:

158	Òbí	ègótégólú		ńnà	'yá	ụ́gbọ̀ànị̀
	Obi	pref-*vb*-ext.suff.-*perf.marker*-ben.extndr. buy		father	pron. him/her	car
	Obi has bought his father a car.					
159	Nwáànyị́	à	é'sírọ́ọ́lụ̀	dí	'yá	ńní
	Woman	this	pref-*vb*-neg.suff-infl.suff-ben.extndr. cook	husband	pron him/her	food
	This woman did not cook for her husband.					
160	Ọ̀	jérọ́ọ́lụ́		ńnẹ́	'yá	ózí
	He/she	*vb*-neg.marker-infl.suff-ben.extndr. go		mother	pron him/her	errand
	He/she did not run errands for his/her mother.					
161	Ụ́mù	ákwụ́kwọ́	èdẹ́gólú		ígwé	ákwụ́kwọ́
	Children	book	pref-*vb*-infl.suff.-*ben.extndr*. write		king	book
	The school children have written to the king.					

162	Ézè	èbídógólú		ń'nwá	yá	áfíá
	Eze	pref-*vb*-perf.marker.-ben.extndr. *start*		child	pron him/her	market
	Eze has started a business for his/her child.					

Table XXXV Constructions where inflectional suffixes precede extensional suffixes

Evidence from the examples (158) – (162) above shows that there is a deviation from the order in the examples (153) – (157), here the inflectional suffixes are systematically followed by the extenders in sentences. A close look at the examples shows that the extenders concerned are all benefactive extenders, and the inflectional suffixes involved are the negative and the perfective suffixes. This is one situation where the extender occurs after the inflectional suffix. Whenever a negative morpheme and a benefactive extender co-occur in the same construction, the inflectional suffix precedes the extender; whenever the perfective suffix and the benefactive extender co-occur in the same construction, the inflectional suffix precedes the extender.

Highlights
In this book, we have been able to document the following:

- a comprehensive description of affixation in the Ọnịcha variety of Igbo.
- the establishment of the vowel /ɛ/ as the phonemic vowel in the Ọnịcha variety of Igbo.
- the confirmation of –LV as the inflectional suffix in Ọnịcha Igbo as opposed to –rV in the Central Igbo variety.
- the status of -kọ as an inflectional suffix marking present imminent in the Ọnịcha Igbo.
- the classification of extensional suffixes attested in Ọnịcha Igbo according to their syntactic and semantic function via the extenders.
- the establishment of the order of extensional suffixes in the variety.
- the recognition of some previously unidentified extensional suffixes in the dialect.

Chapter 6

Auxiliaries in Igbo

6. Introduction

The term "auxiliary", according to Crystal (1997:35), is used in the grammatical classification of verbs to refer to the set of verbs, subordinate to the main lexical verbs, which help to make distinctions in mood, aspect, voice, etc. Linguists, including Quirk et al (1972:65), describe auxiliary verbs in English as helping verbs. Lester (1976:49) classifies English auxiliary verbs as verbs because they can have tense markers attached to them in the same way as the main verbs. Okiwelu (1979:13) defines auxiliarization as:

> "...le procédé progressif selon lequel le contenu sémantique d'un verbe est réduit au profit d'un autre verbe." [...the process by which the semantic content of a verb is progressively reduced for the benefit of another verb].

Ndimele (1996:64; 1999:103) groups auxiliary verbs in the English language into two parts:

- primary auxiliary verbs (do, have, be)
- modal auxiliary verbs (can/could, shall/should, may/might, must, ought to, used to, need, dare).

He lists the following as functions of auxiliary verbs in the English language:

- in Yes/No questions, the auxiliary verbs are used for querying.
- it bears tense or aspect marking in place of main verbs.
- the auxiliary verb helps in reducing monotony – enables the speaker to avoid repeating the main verbs or the entire verb phrase.
- sometimes, the auxiliary verb replaces the main verb, which is only understood from the context.

The objective of this section is to present, in a systematic manner, the different auxiliary constructions and their uses in the generalized Ọnịcha dialect of Igbo, and secondly, to examine the effect of the co-occurrence of the auxiliaries and the perfective verb forms in the dialect.

The auxiliary is here presented in two parts part 1 discusses auxiliaries and their uses in simple constructions in Ọnịcha Igbo. Part 2 discusses the use of auxiliaries in the perfective constructions in the Ọnịcha Igbo variety.

Okafor (2000:48) argues that the use of the term auxiliary verb in the analysis of the Igbo verbal system has blurred the true picture of the morpho-syntactic behaviour of the linguistic elements operating in the Igbo verbal system. He prefers the term verbal modifying element because, according to him, it presents a true picture of the rule-governed morpho-syntactic relationship existing between the main verb and other linguistic elements found in the verbal system of Igbo language. Green and Igwe (1963:141) recognize one true auxiliary verb – *na* in Igbo. This auxiliary is equivalent to what Ndimele refers to as primary auxiliary. Emenanjo (1976:38) recognizes six auxiliary verbs in the Ọnịcha dialect of Igbo. They are:

- na   marks durative/progressive affirmative
- di   marks durative/progressive negative
- ga   marks future affirmative
- ma   marks future negative
- ga ~-ka   marks the perfective negative
- ga ~-ka   marks the unfulfilled.

Following Ndimele's method of classification, the auxiliary verbs in the Ọnịcha Igbo will be grouped in this book into:

- Primary auxiliary   -na (affirmative)
                       -dị (negative)

- Modal auxiliary   -ga (affirmative)
                       -ma (negative)
                       -ka (perfective affirmative)
                       -ka (perfective negative)
                       -ka (unfulfilled marker)

For simplicity and clarity, the two groups of auxiliaries just mentioned will be studied as follows:

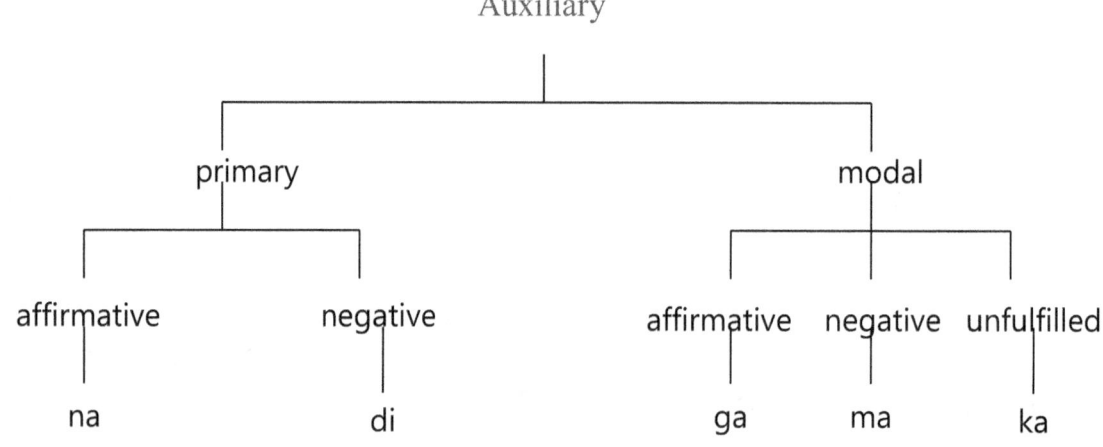

In what follows, we shall discuss, with examples, the above auxiliary verbs in the Ọnịcha Igbo.

Affixation and Auxiliaries in Igbo 135

6.1 Primary Auxiliary

The primary auxiliary verb in Ọnịcha is used to express a progressive action (action that goes on at the moment of speaking) or a habitual action (action that goes on repeatedly). In the Ọnịcha dialect of Igbo, the primary auxiliary may be expressed in the affirmative or negative form.

Affirmative Primary Auxiliary 'na'

The affirmative primary auxiliary in the Ọnịcha Igbo is 'na'. It can express an action that is on-going at the time of speaking, or an action that takes place habitually. The following examples explicate the different uses of the affirmative primary auxiliary.

1. Òbí nà-èjέ ákwụ́kwọ́
   Obi aux.-participle book
        prog.-going
   Obi is going to school/Obi is a student.

2. Fá nà-èsí ń'ní
   They prog.-cooking food
   They cook/They are cooking/They are cooks.

3. Ọ́ nà-àjọ́ ń'jọ́
   He/she aux.-participle badness
          prog.-being bad
   He/she is stingy/uncharitable.

4. Ànyí nà-ázà ụ́nọ̀
   We aux.-participle house
       prog.-sweeping
   We sweep the house/We are sweeping the house/We are sweepers.

From the above examples, it is observed that the auxiliary verb 'na' is always followed by the participle. The context and situation determine whether the action being expressed is progressive or habitual. The tone of the auxiliary is consistently low.

Negative Primary Auxiliary dí

The negative primary auxiliary in Ọnịcha Igbo is –dí. Just like the affirmative primary auxiliary, the negative primary auxiliary can express either a progressive negative action (action that is not on-going at the moment of speaking) or a habitual action (action that does not go on repeatedly). The general negative marker in the Ọnịcha variety of Igbo is =rọ, which is attached to the verb root whenever negation is intended or expressed. When the verb root is preceded by a negative auxiliary verb, the negative inflection marking is attached on the negative auxiliary. But in synchronic usage, the inflectional negative marker =rọ is deleted in the surface structure, leaving only the negative auxiliary verb =di to fulfill the function of the negative structure marking. We shall, hereafter, give examples using both the underlying and the surface structure realizations of the negative primary auxiliary in Ọnịcha Igbo.

	UNDERLYING/DEEP STRUCTURE		SURFACE STRUCTURE
5a	Àdá á'dị̀rọ-ànụ́ í'fɛ́ Ada pref-<u>neg.aux</u>-neg.suff- *participle* thing Ada is disobedient/Ada does not hear/Ada is deaf	5b	Àdá á'dị́-ànụ́ í'fɛ́ Ada pref-<u>aux</u>.-*participle* thing neg.-*hearing* Ada is not obedient/ Ada does not hear (≈ Ada is deaf).
6a	Ànyị́ á'dị́rọ́-èzú ó'rí We pref-<u>neg.aux</u>-neg.suff- *participle*-<u>theft</u> We do not steal/We are not thieves	6b	Ànyị́ á'dị́-èzú ó'rí We pref-<u>aux</u>.-*participle* theft neg.-*stealing* We do not steal/We are not thieves.
7a	Úchè á'dị́rọ́-èkwú ó'kwú Uche pref-<u>neg.aux</u>-neg.suff- *participle*-<u>speech</u> Uche is not speaking/Uche does not speak (≈ Uche is dumb).	7b	Úchè á'dị́-èkwú ó'kwú Uche pref-<u>aux</u>.-*participle* speech neg.-*speaking* Uche is not speaking/Uche does not speak (≈ Uche is dumb).
8a	Ọ̀ dị́'rọ́ ázà únọ̀ He/she <u>neg.aux</u>-neg.suff *participle* house He/she is not sweeping the house/He\she does not sweep the house	8b	Ọ̀ dị́ ázà únọ̀ He/she <u>aux.neg</u>-*participle* house *sweeping* He/she is not sweeping the house/He\she does not sweep the house

Considering the above structures (deep and surface structure realizations), it is observed that the negative suffix =rọ, which is realized in negative structures (structures without auxiliary verbs) in Ọnịcha Igbo, is deleted in the surface structure. The same thing applies to the modal negative auxiliary. Our conclusion in this section, therefore, is that negative markings in the Ọnịcha Igbo variety are borne by the negative auxiliary alone. In other words, the negative suffix does not function together with the negative auxiliary verb in the Ọnịcha Igbo as observed above. It is also observed that, as in the affirmative auxiliary constructions, the negative auxiliary always precedes the participle. It is observed that, while the affirmative primary auxiliary does not take a verbal vowel prefix for any type of subject, the negative primary auxiliary takes a verbal vowel prefix for subject nouns and plural pronouns but omits it for singular pronouns. Each of the sentences above can be interpreted in at least two different ways: either as a process that goes on or does not go on at the moment of speaking, or as an action that does not happen repeatedly. Some of the sentences can even be interpreted idiomatically as the glosses above show.

6.2 Modal Auxiliary

Ejele (2004:851), quoting Quirk and Greenbaum (1973), Quirk et al (1980), describes modality as expressions indicating obligation, probability, and possibility. Modality is, as a matter of fact, described by linguists as the attitude of the speaker towards what he/she is saying. Following the above description of modality, this paper regards modal auxiliary as the helping verb that co-occurs with the main verb to express obligation, ability, permission, probability, intention. Modal auxiliaries can be used in expressing both the affirmative and the negative, with perfective notions, just as the primary auxiliaries are used above in expressing affirmative and negative realities. They cannot occur in a sentence without a main verb. The following are examples of the auxiliarization of modals in the expressions of different notions.

Affirmative Modal Auxiliary Verbs

The affirmative modal auxiliary verb in Ọnịcha dialect of Igbo is denoted by 'gà'. The following are examples of sentences that express modality in the affirmative in Ọnịcha Igbo.

9. Ézè gà-àgbá é'gwú
   Eze m.aux-participle dance
   dancing
   Eze will dance.

10. Únù gà-ánọ̀ n'ụ́nọ̀
    You(pl) m.aux-participle prep.-house
    staying in
    You will stay in the house.

11. Fá gà-àkwụ́ ụ́'gwọ́
    They m.aux-participle debt
    paying
    They will pay.

12. Ọ́ gà-èbú íbù
    He/she m.aux-participle fatness
    being fat
    He/she will be fat.

It is observed from the above examples that the modal auxiliary verbs can co-occur with both active and stative verbs. In the Ọnịcha Igbo, the same modal auxiliary verb can be used to express different notions: possibility, obligation, permission, ability, certainty, or even intention. It is the context and situation that can limit the semantic reference of the modal auxiliary in the Ọnịcha Igbo. The four sentences above can therefore express any semantic notion in the Ọnịcha Igbo. But all the sentences express prospective notions. It is observed from the examples above that the tone of the affirmative modal auxiliary verb in the Ọnịcha dialect is consistently low.

Negative Modal Auxiliary Verbs
The negative modal auxiliary verb in Ọnịcha is denoted by 'ma'. The following are examples of negative modal auxiliary verbs in Ọnịcha Igbo constructions:

13. Àdá   á'má   élí   ń'ní
    Ada   pref-neg.m.aux.   participle   food
                                eating

    Ada will not eat.

14. Íbè   á'má   ébí   n'é'nú
    Ibe   pref-neg.m.aux.   participle   prep-up
                                living   in

    Ibe will not live upstairs.

15. Ọ̀   má   'álárụ́   ụ́'lá
    He/she   neg.m.aux.   participle   sleep
                                sleeping

    He/she will not sleep.

It is observed that, like every other auxiliary verb, the negative modal auxiliary verb is always followed by a participle. It takes a verbal vowel prefix when the subject of the construction is either a noun or a plural pronoun. With a singular subject pronoun, the modal auxiliary verb does not take any verbal vowel prefix. The tone of the negative modal auxiliary is high when the subject of the construction is a singular pronoun, but is reduced to a downstep when the subject of the sentence is a plural pronoun or a proper noun.

For the semantic interpretation, the negative modal auxiliary 'ma' can be used to express any of the semantic notions listed above (ability, probability, possibility, etc.) with respect to the context.

6.2.1 Modal Auxiliary and Perfective Verbs Forms
It has earlier been pointed out that modal auxiliary co-occurs with the main verb to yield the semantic notions of possibility, ability, probability, certainty, etc. Effort has been made in section A to show the process of auxiliarization in Ọnịcha Igbo.
In this section, the effect of the co-occurrence of the modal auxiliaries and the perfective verb forms will be examined. The affirmative and negative modal auxiliaries have been discussed above. In what follows, the unfulfilled modal auxiliaries (affirmative and negative) will be examined and discussed under the following headings:

- the future perfective affirmative
- the future perfective negative
- the unfulfilled perfective affirmative
- the unfulfilled perfective negative

The Future Perfective Affirmative

The future perfective affirmative in Ọnịcha is expressed via a combination of the affirmative modal auxiliary 'ga', followed by the participial prefix affixed to the verb to which is suffixed the perfective suffix –go. The following are examples of the affirmative perfective constructions in Ọnịcha Igbo:

16. Àmáká   gà   èsígó   'jí
    Amaka   m.aux.participle-<u>perf.suff.</u> yam
                             cooking
    Amaka will/must have cooked yam.

17. Fá   gà   àwụ́gó   'árụ̀
    They   m.aux.participle-<u>perf.suff.</u> body
                             bathing
    They will/must have taken their bath.

18. Íbè   gà   ázàgó   ụ́nọ̀
    Ibe   m.aux.participle-<u>perf.suff.</u> house
                             sweeping
    Ibe will/must have swept the house.

19. Úchè   gà   èbígó   'Ábá
    Uche   m.aux.participle-<u>perf.suff.</u> Aba
                             living
    Uche will/must have lived at Aba.

From the examples above, it is observed that the affirmative modal auxiliary verb 'ga' which functions as a simple modal/future/anticipative auxiliary verb in the prospective construction above is now functioning as a modalizer because of the presence of the perfective suffix –go.

The perfective suffix has only one form in Ọnịcha Igbo. It co-occurs with both expanded and non-expanded vowels. The auxiliary 'ga' maintains a low tone in all the constructions in which it appeared above. In the Ọnịcha Igbo, it is observed that the perfective suffix is affixed to the participle, while in the Central Igbo dialect, it is affixed to the auxiliary. The tone of the perfective suffix is invariable in Ọnịcha Igbo; it is consistently high in all the data given above. All the constructions above are hypothetical.

The Future Perfective Negative

The future perfective negative in Ọnịcha Igbo is formed by the combination of the negative auxiliary 'ma', followed by the participial prefix attached to the verb to which is suffixed the perfective suffix –go. The following are some examples:

20. Fà á'má égógó 'jí
    They pref.-neg.m.aux. participle-<u>perf.suff.</u> yam
    buying
    They will/must not have bought yam.

21. Íké á'má ásụ́gọ́ ákwà
    Ike pref.-neg.m.aux. participle-<u>perf.suff.</u> cloth
    washing
    Ike will/must not have washed cloth.

22. Úchè á'má ébígó 'Ábá
    Uche pref.-neg.m.aux. participle-<u>perf.suff.</u> Aba
    living
    Uche will/must not have lived at Aba.

23. Ọ̀ má ázàgọ́ ụ́nọ̀
    He/she pref.-neg.m.aux. participle-<u>perf.suff.</u> house
    sweeping
    He/she will/must not have swept the house.

From the above examples, it is observed that the negative auxiliary verb 'má' has a consistently step tone. With a noun or a plural pronoun subject, the tone on the negative auxiliary verb is reduced to downstep. The tone of the perfective suffix –go is consistently high. The co-occurrence of the modal auxiliary with future modals yields hypothetical statements as observed in the examples above.

The Unfulfilled Perfective Affirmative

The unfulfilled perfective affirmative construction in Ọnịcha dialect of Igbo is a construction where the desire or hope expressed by the verb has not been realized, even though it is supposed to have been accomplished before the moment of speaking. It is formed by a combination of the unfulfilled marker –ka (henceforth um) and the verb root. When the unfulfilled marker is followed by the verb root to which the participial prefix a=/e=/ɛ= and the perfective suffix –go are respectively affixed, an unfulfilled perfective construction results. Here are some examples:

24. Àdá 'áká 'élígó ńní
    Ada pref.-um participle-<u>perf.suff.</u> food
    eating
    Ada should have eaten.

25.	Fá	'áká	'ákwúgó	ú'gwó
	They	pref.-um	participle-<u>perf.suff.</u> paying	payment

They should have paid.

26.	Ó	'ká	àzàgò	únò
	He/she	um	participle-<u>perf.suff.</u> sweeping	house

He/she should have swept the house.

27.	Únù	àká	àkògó	jí
	You(pl.)	pref.-um	participle-<u>perf.suff.</u> planting	yam

You should have planted yam.

It is observed from the above data that the unfulfilled perfective marker co-occurs with perfective verb forms to produce hypothetical sentences. For instance, the sentences above have not been accomplished before the moment of speaking because of the presence of the unfulfilled marker 'ka'. Just as in previous examples, the unfulfilled marker always precedes the participle. The perfective suffix –go copies the tone of the verb root to which it is attached, as can be seen in the examples.

The Unfulfilled Perfective Negative

The unfulfilled perfective negative in Ọnịcha Igbo is formed when the perfective marker 'ka' is followed by the verb root to which are affixed the participial prefix a=/e=/ɛ= and the negative suffix =rọ. The following are some of the examples of the unfulfilled perfective negative constructions in Ọnịcha Igbo:

28.	Íbè	á'ká	èlíró	ń'ní
	Ibe	pref.-um	participle-<u>perf.suff.</u> eating	food

Ibe has not yet eaten (food).

29.	Ànyị	á'ká	ázàró	únò
	We	pref.-um	participle-<u>perf.suff.</u> sweeping	house

We have not yet swept the house.

30.	Ọ̀	ká	àkwúró	ú'gwó
	He/she	um	participle-<u>perf.suff.</u> paying	payment

He/she has not yet paid.

31.	Ì	ká	àmùró		ákwúkwó
	You(sing.)	um	participle-<u>perf.suff.</u>		book
			learning		

You have not yet studied.

From the above examples, we observe the tonal morphology of the unfulfilled marker; it is high when it co-occurs with singular subject pronouns, but it is downstepped when it co-occurs with noun subjects or plural pronouns. The participial prefix has low tone for high tone verb roots and high tone for low tone verb roots. The present perfective negative and the unfulfilled perfective negative are expressed in exactly the same way in the Ọnịcha dialect. Both are expressed as above.

6.3 Conclusion

We have, with substantial amount of data in the first section of this book described and analyzed affixation in the Ọnịcha variety of Igbo. In the procedure of analysis, the functional criterion of classification of affixes is applied thereby using the three clear-cut divisions of affixes thus: inflectional affixes, derivational affixes, and extensional affixes.

Each division of affixes is further organized into sections for easy analysis and description. The processes of prefixation, interfixation, circumfixation, deverbalization, and tonology are discussed under derivational affixes. For instance, the derivation of infinitive and participle is considered under prefixation. All other derivations involving prefixation are also considered under prefixation. Such derivations include reduplication (total and partial).
Under interfixation, the derivatives are grouped according to their base formatives. For example, the derivatives that have nouns as their base are discussed under noun-base form derivatives, while those that have verbs as their base are considered under verb-base form derivatives. It is discovered that the verb-base form of derivational affixes are more productive than the noun-base form in Ọnịcha.
The derivational functions of tone are studied in the book using the associative and determinative constructions to distinguish between tonal functions in the given constructions. With respect to the functions of tones in the derivation of nominals from sentences, the derivations of personal names from Igbo sentences and phrases are illustrated with examples.

With respect to inflections, it is observed that affixes are indispensable in inflectional markings in the Ọnịcha Igbo. Nominals are, however, not inflected in Igbo, but a few nouns in Ọnịcha exchange their initial high-back vowel 'o' with non-back vowel 'i'. The entire inflectional markings are achieved with affixes.
In discussing extensional suffixes, different examples are provided to differentiate verb root and enclitics from derivational, inflectional, and extensional suffixes. A classification of extensional suffixes frequently attested in the Ọnịcha dialect is

provided, and some examples are generated to show their application. At the end of the analysis, and with the help of a grid which we have also generated, the co-occurrence possibilities of extensional suffixes and the internal constraints governing them are examined. Examining the order of extensional and inflectional suffixes, it was observed that each suffix has its own particular position in a construction. The order brings the extensional suffix closer to the verb root than the inflectional ones. This is the structure in all the Ọnịcha Igbo constructions except in constructions involving negative morphemes together with benefactive extenders. The perfective and negative constructions (involving benefactive extenders) are mostly affected as our examples show.

In the second section of the book, we examined the functioning of auxiliaries in Ọnịcha through the process of auxiliarization. Several constructions were considered using different data. From our analysis, it was discovered that the primary auxiliary verbs express habitual or progressive actions, pure and simple, while modal auxiliary verbs combine with perfective verb forms to express different nuances as observed in the examples. For instance, the modal auxiliary verb with future modals (affirmative and negative) expresses hypotheses (obligation, possibilities, necessity, etc.). The modal auxiliary verb with perfective verb forms (affirmative and negative) express unfulfilled actions. One of the highlights of this study is that the negative auxiliary verbs are self-sufficient in expressing negation in the Ọnịcha Igbo variety; they do not take the negative suffix.

References

Abraham, R.C. (1967). *The principles of Ibo.* Ibadan: Occasional Publications.

Adam, R.F.G. (1932). *A modern Igbo gammar.* London: Oxford University Press.

Afigbo, A.E. (1986). *An outline of Igbo history.* Owerri: Rada Publishing Company

Allerton, D.J. (1997). *Essentials of grammatical theory.* London: Routledge and Kegan Paul.

Anagbogu, P.N. (1990). *The grammar of Igbo nominalizations.* Onitsha: University Publishing Company.

Anagbogu, P.N. (2000). The semantic link in Igbo nominal compounding. *Journal of the Linguistic Association of Nigeria,* No. 7.

Anyaehie, E.O. (1995). *Les affixes en morphosyntaxe Igbo.* Okigwe: Fasmen Communications.

Bauer, L. (1983). *English word-formation.* Cambridge: Cambridge University Press.

Bendor-Samuel, J. (1989). *The Niger-Congo languages.* Lanham: University Press of America.

Bled, E.O. (1954). *Cours Superieur d'othorgraphe.* Paris: Classiques Hachette.

Bloomfield, L (1933). *Language.* London: University of Chicago Press.

Boyd, R. (1989). Adamawa Ubangi, In Bendor-Samuel, J. (ed.). *The Niger-Congo languages.* New York: University of America.

Bybee, J.L. (1985). *Morphology: A study of the relation between meaning and form.* Amsterdam/Philadelphia: John Benjamins Publishing Company.

Carrel, P.A. (1970). *Igbo transformational grammar.* West African Language Monograph 8 Cambridge: Cambridge University Press.

Chafe, W.L. (1970). *Meaning and the structure of language.* London: The University of Chicago Press.

Clark, M.M. (1990). *The tonal system of Igbo.* Dordrecht: Foris Publications.

Comrie, B. (1976). *Aspect. An introduction to the study of verbal aspects and related problems.* Cambridge: Cambridge University Press.

Comrie, B. (1985). *Tense.* Canbridge: Cambridge University Press.

Creissels, D. (1989). *Aperçu sur les structures phonologiques des langues negro-aficaines.* Grenoble: Ellug.

Crystal, D. (1995). *The Cambridge encyclopedia of the English language.* Cambridge: Cambridge University Press.

Crystal, D. (1997). *The dictionary of linguistics and phonetics.* 4th ed. Oxford: Blackwell Publishers.

Echeruo, M. (1998). *Igbo-English dictionary of the Igbo language.* London: Yale University Press.

Ejele, P.E. (1996). *An introductory course on language.* Port Harcourt: University of Port Harcourt Press.

Ejele, P.E. (2000). Temporal distinctions as bases for the semantic classification of verbs. Insights from Esan. *Kiabara Journal of Humanities,* Volume 6, No. 2. Pp 43-54.

Ejele, P.E. (2004). The expression of mood and modality. In *Language and culture in Nigeria: A festschrift for Okon Essien* ed. by Ozo-Mekuri Ndimele. Aba: National Institute for Nigerian Languages (NINLAN) 851-867.

Ejele, P.E. (2005). Word formation processes in Esan. In *Globalization and the study of languages in Africa.* ed. by Ozo-Mekuri Ndimele. Port Harcourt: Grand Orbit Communications and Emhai Press. Pp. 313-328.

Ejiofor, L.U. (1982). *Igbo kingdoms, power and control.* Onitsha: Africana Publishers Ltd.

Eka, D. (2004). *Elements of grammar and mechanics of the English language.* Uyo: Samuf (Nigeria).

Eke, U.K. (1985). *Elements de description de l'Igbo d'Ohafia. phonologie, système nominal, elements de relation.* Thèse de Doctorat de Troisième Cycle. Grenoble : Universite de Grenoble III.

Emenanjo, E.N. (1973). Towards definite Igbo dictionaries. A review of Williamson's Igbo-English dictionary. *Ikenga.* Volume 2. No.2.

Emenanjo, E.N. (1975a). *The Igbo verbal: A descriptive analysis.* Unpublished M.A. Dissertation in the Department of Linguistics and Nigerian Languages, University of Ibadan.

Emenanjo, E.N. (1975b). Igbo grammar. In *Igbo Language and culture.* Ibadan: Oxford University Press, 85-95.

Emenanjo, E.N. (1975c). Aspects of the Igbo verb. In *Igbo language and culture.* Ibadan: Oxford University Press, 160-170.

Emenanjo, E.N. (1976). *Aspects of the phonology and morphophonemics of Onitsha.* (A dialect of Igbo). Department of Linguistics. University of Ibadan.

Emenanjo, E.N. (1978). *Elements of modern Igbo grammar.* Ibadan: Oxford University Press.

Emenanjo, E.N. (1982a). The Interfix: An aspect of universal morphology. *Journal of West African Languages.* Volume XII, No. 1.

Emenanjo, E.N. (1982b). Suffixes and enclitics in Igbo. In *Igbo language and culture.* Volume 2. Ibadan: University Press Limited.

Emenanjo, E.N. (1983). Verb derivational morphology. In *Reading on Igbo verbs.* ed. by Nwachukwu, P.A. University of Nigeria, Nsukka.

Essien, O.E. (1990). *A grammar of the Ibibio language.* Ibadan: University Press Ltd.

Green, M.M. & G.E. Igwe. (1963). *A descriptive grammar of Igbo.* London: Oxford University Press.

Henderson, R.N. (1972). *The king in every man.* New Haven and London: Yale University Press.

Hocket, C.F. (1958). *A course in modern linguistics.* New York: Macmillan Company.

Huddleston, R. (1984). *Introduction to the grammar of English.* Cambridge: Cambridge University Press.

Igwe, G.E. (1975). Igbo: A tone language. In *Igbo language and culture.* Ibadan: Oxford University Press, 95-103.

Igwe, G.E. (1999). *Igbo-English dictionary.* Ibadan: University Press Plc.

Igwe, G.E. & M.M. Green (1964). *A short Igbo grammar*. Ibadan: Oxford University Press.
Isichei, E. (1977). *Igbo worlds*. London and Basingstoke: Macmillan Sentences.
Kari, E.E. (1995). Extensional suffixes in Degema. *AAP* No. 44, 149-168
Katamba, F. (1993). *Morphology*. London: Macmillan Press.
Kelly, B.J. (1954). *An introduction to Onitsha Igbo*. London: Macmillan & Co. Publishers.
Lester, M. (1976). *Introductory transformational grammar of English*. Holt, Rinehart and Winston.
Lyons, J. (1968). *Introduction to theoretical linguistics*. London: Cambridge University Press.
Matthews, P.H. (1974). *Morphology: An introduction to the theory of word-structure*. London: Cambridge University Press.
Mitterand, H. (1969). *A.B.C. de grammaire Française*. Paris: Fernand Nathan.
Ndimele, O.-M. (1996). *An advanced English grammar and usage*. Revised ed. Aba: NINLAN Books.
Ndimele, O.-M. (1999). *A first course on morphology and syntax*. Port Harcourt: Emhai Publishing.
Ndimele, O.-M. (2003). *A concise grammar and lexicon of Echie*. Aba: NINLAN
Ndimele, O.-M. (2003). On the wh-parameter and grammar induction. Insights from African languages. In *Four decades of languages and linguistics in Nigeria: A festschrift for Kay Williamson*. ed. by Ozo-Mekuri Ndimele.
Newmeyer, F.I. (1990). *Linguistics: The Cambridge survey*. Cambridge: Cambridge University Press.
Ngoesi, M.C. (2000). *Nchikota ihe omumu nke asusu Igbo*. Nkpor: Optimal Press.
Noss, P.A. (1991). *Gbaya, phonologie et grammaire dialect yaa Nuwe*. Eglise Evangelique Lutherienne du Cameroun. Centre de la traduction Gbaya Meigang.
Nwachukwu, P. A. (1983) ed. *Readings on the Igbo Verbs*. Onitsha: Africana-FEP Publishers
Nwachukwu, P. A. (1984). Stative Verbs in Igbo Syntax. *Journal of West African Languages* XIV, 2, 81-99.
Nwachukwu, P. A. (1987). *The Argument Structure of Igbo Verbs*. Lexicon Project Center for Cognitive Science. Massachusetts: The M.I.T. Press.
Nwadike, I. U. (1981). *The Development of Written Igbo as a School Subject*. New York: University of New York.
Nwagu, L. U. (1992). *Lexical Variation Between the Onitsha and Awka Dialects of Igbo*. Unpublished B.A. Thesis. University of Port Harcourt.
Nwigwe, N. (1996). *Prefixation in Ngwa Igbo Verb Morphology*. Unpublished M.A. Thesis. University of Port Harcourt.
Nwigwe, N. (1997). Perfect: A Grammatical Category in Igbo. Nigerian Language Studies. No. 5, Pp 18-24.

Nwigwe, N. (2003). *Mood and Modality in Ngwa Igbo*. Unpublished PhD Dissertation in the Department of Linguistics and Communication Studies. University of Port Harcourt.

Ogbalu, F. C. (1975). *Igbo Spelling in Igbo Language & Culture*. Ibadan: Oxford University Press.

Ogwueleka, O. (1995). *The Syntax and Semantics of the Stator in Igbo*. Nigerian Language Studies. No.3, Pp 20-30.

Ojiaku Ezike, P. A. (1989). *Fonoloji na Utoasusu Igbo*. Lagos: Macmillan Publishers.

Okafor, M. I. (2000). *The Non-Relevance of the Auxiliary Approach in the Analysis of Igbo Grammar*. APNILAC.

Okeke, V. O. (1984). *Key to Igbo Language*. Obosi: Pacific College Press Ltd.

Okiwelu, B. (1979). *Le Processus d'Auxiliarisation en Français*. Grenoble :Université des Langues et Lettres de Grenoble III.

Okolo, B. A. (1995). Shifting Moods in Igbo Oral Discourse. Nigerian Language Studies. No. 3,Pp 31-39. NINLAN.

Okonkwo, M. N. (1974). *A Complete Course in Igbo Grammar*. Lagos: Macmillan Publishers.

Okoye, B. I. (1998). *Negation in the Onitsha Dialect of Igbo*. Unpublished B.A. Thesis. Uniport.

Onukawa, M. C. (1994) A Reclassification of the Igbo-rV suffixes. Nigerian Language Studies. No.2, Pp 81-91.Aba.

Onukawa, M. C. (1995). A Re-analysis of the So-called Igbo De-sentential Nominals. In *Issues in African Languages and Linguistics. Essays in Honour of Kay Williamson* ed. by E.N. Emenanjo & Ozo-Mekuri Ndimele. Aba: NINLAN Books. Pp 266-278.

Onukawa, M.C. (1996a). Aspects of the semantics of Igbo deverbative reduplicated nouns. *Nigerian Language Studies* No. 4, Pp. 36-42.

Onukawa, M.C. (1996b). Suffixation in Igbo derivational morphology – A diachronic study. In *Language Studies and Relevance 2* ed. by Evaristus O. Anyaehie and Amechi Ihenacho. Uturu: Language Centre Publications.

Onukawa, M.C. (1997). Studies on Interfixation in Igbo: Another Dimension. *Journal of Nigerian Languages and Literatures*. No. 5. Lincom International, Department of African Linguistics. Unterschleissheim/Munchen. Pp 1-7.

Onukawa, M.C. (1999a). On the concept of circumfixation in Igbo. *Ihafa: A Journal of African Studies*. Vol. III No. 1 Pp. 119-132.

Onukawa, M.C. (1999b). The Order of Extensional Suffixes in Igbo. *AAP* No. 59 pp. 109-129.

Onukawa, M.C. (2000). Aspects of the semantics of the Igbo deverbative reduplicated noun. *Jolan* No. 7.

Onukawa, M.C. (2002). Radical elements in Igbo diachronic derivational morphology. *African Journal of Language Research* Vol. 1, Nos 1 & 2, Pp 43-50.

Onumajuru, E.M. (1985). *Système verbal de la langue Igbo (Le parler d'Orlu)*. Lille: Universite de Lille III.

Onumajuru, E.M. (1998). Attitudes of the Igbos towards their language: Problems and prospects. Volume 2. Ikot Ekpene: *Annang Minorities Studies Association.*

Onumajuru, V.C. (2005). A comparative study of Ọnịcha and Central Igbo varieties. In *Trends in the study of languages and linguistics in Nigeria. A festschrift for Philip Akujuobi Nwachukwu.* ed. by Ozo-Mekuri Ndimele. Port Harcourt: Grand Orbit Communications & Emhai Press, Pp. 691-701.

Onuora, N. (1997). *The Chima Dynasty in Ọnịcha.* Lagos: John Peterson Enterprises.

Onwuejeogwu, M.A. (1975). The Igbo culture area. In *Igbo Language and Culture.* Ibadan: Oxford University Press.

Onwukeme, J.N. (2001). *Suffixes in Nnobi-Igbo.* Unpublished M.A. Thesis. University of Port Harcourt.

Quirk, R. and S. Greenbaum (1973). A *university grammar of English.* London: Longman.

Quirk, R. & S. Greenbaum (1985). *A Grammar of Contemporary English.* London: Longman.

Radford, A. (1988). *Tranformational grammar. A first course.* Cambridge: Cambridge University Press.

Radford, A. et al. (1999). *Linguistics: An introduction.* Cambridge: Cambridge University Press.

Rodman, R. & V. Fromkin. (1998). *An introduction to language,* Sixth edition. Forth Worth: Harcourt Brace College Publishers.

Spencer, A. (1991). *Morphological theory.* Oxford: Blackwell Publishers.

Tomori, S.H. (1977). *The morphology and syntax of present day English: An introduction.* London: Heinemann Educational Books Ltd.

Trask, R.L. (1993). *A Dictionary of grammatical terms in linguistics.* London & New York: Routledge.

Uchendu, V.C. (1965). *The Igbo of South East Nigeria.* U.S.A: Rinehart and Winston.

Uwalaka, M.A. (1997). *Igbo grammar.* Ibadan: The Pen Services

Uwalaka, M.A. (1997). *Ahiriokwu Igbo.* Ibadan: Kraft Books.

Uwasomba, B.U. (1998). *Interfixes and derivational suffixes in Ibere-Ikwuano Igbo.* Unpublished M.A. Thesis. University of Port Harcourt.

Ward, I.C.N. (1936). *An introduction to the Ibo language.* Cambridge: Heffer.

Welmers, W.E. (1973). *African language structures.* London: University of California Press.

Williamson, Kay (1972). *Igbo-English dictionary.* Benin-City: Ethiope Publishing Company.

Williamson, Kay (1984). *Practical orthography in Nigeria.* Ibadan: Heinemann Educational Books (Nig).

Yul-Ifode, S. (2005). Affixation in Isoko. In *Globalization & the study of languages in Africa.* ed. by Ozo-Mekuri Ndimele. Port Harcourt: Grand Orbit Communications & Emhai Press. Pp 305-311.

Subject Index

Active Verb, 27
Advanced Root Tongue, 7
Affixation, 11, 12, 13, 14, 17, 20, 25, 29, 30, 42, 56, 69, 131, 142
Agentive, 78, 79, 92
Agreement, 19
Allomorphs, 21
Allophones, 6, 7
Anteriority, 33, 55, 95, 101
Aorist, 38
Applicative, 36, 39, 40, 103, 125
Aspiration, 5, 8, 29
Base, 12, 14, 15, 23, 24, 26, 29, 31, 32, 37, 61, 69, 71, 72, 77, 79, 81, 84, 85, 87, 95, 97, 142
Benefactive, 36, 39, 40, 41, 95, 107, 108, 114, 124, 128, 131, 143
Bound Cognate Noun (Bcn), 25, 74
Causative, 96, 118, 119
Circumfix, 15, 22
Circumfixation, 20, 24, 61, 69, 73, 142
Circumfixation, 61, 73
Class-Changing, 11, 12
Class-Maintaining, 11, 32, 36
Clitic, 98
Complement, 23, 24, 25, 34, 44, 45, 62, 65, 66, 74, 75, 76, 78, 79, 80, 81, 94
Complementary Distribution, 6
Complex Gerunds, 77
Compounding, 11, 12, 13
Dative, 95, 105, 106, 124
Derivation, 6, 11, 12, 13, 16, 17, 19, 22, 24, 25, 26, 29, 30, 31, 32, 34, 61, 62, 68, 69, 70, 71, 72, 73, 78, 83, 86, 87, 93, 94, 142
Derivational, 14, 15, 16, 17, 18, 19, 24, 29, 30, 31, 32, 33, 36, 61, 62, 66, 69, 71, 78, 79, 91, 96, 142, 143
Derivational Morphology, 30
Deverbatives, 29, 30, 61, 74, 83
Downstep, 9, 47, 49, 51, 63, 78, 88, 138, 140
Durative, 46, 95, 102, 103, 125, 134
Enclitics, 32, 95, 98, 99, 143
Enclitics, 96, 98, 99
Expanded Vowels, 6, 7, 42, 44, 58, 84, 100, 118
Extenders, 95, 96, 99, 100, 101, 102, 103, 104, 105, 106, 107, 108, 109, 110, 111, 112, 113, 114, 115, 116, 117, 118, 119, 121, 122, 125, 128, 129, 131, 143
Extensional, 8, 15, 27, 29, 30, 32, 33, 35, 36, 54, 55, 64, 95, 96, 97, 98, 99, 101, 102, 108, 121, 123, 124, 125, 126, 127, 128, 129, 130, 131, 142, 143
Extensional Affixes, 95, 142
Extensional Suffixes, 35, 95, 98, 99, 123, 126
Factative, 27, 28, 38
Fixative, 95, 109, 110
Form Class, 12, 25
Frequentative, 95, 102, 125
Future Affirmative, 49, 50, 134
Future Negative, 50, 51, 134
Gender, 19, 37
Genitive, 19, 87
Gerund, 25, 77
Gerundive Nominals, 31
Glottal Sound, 8
Imminent Negative, 45, 48, 49
Imperative Affirmative, 42, 43
Imperative Negative, 44
Inchoactive, 95, 100
Indicative, 27, 31, 35, 37, 38, 39, 40, 48, 57, 76, 98, 102, 105, 106, 109, 112, 114, 115
Infinitive, 23, 25, 30, 48, 61, 62, 63, 64, 65, 66, 68, 69, 93, 124, 142
Infix, 15, 22
Infixation, 20
Inflection, 11, 13, 16, 17, 18, 19, 34, 35, 37, 41, 136
Inflectional, 14, 15, 16, 17, 18, 19, 25, 27, 29, 30, 32, 33, 34, 35, 36, 37, 39, 57, 66, 67, 96, 97, 98, 108, 113, 114, 115, 125, 129, 130, 131, 136, 142, 143
Inflectional Affixes, 34, 38, 41, 42, 45, 51
Interfix, 15, 22, 32, 72
Interfixation, 20, 32, 61, 71, 72, 93, 142
Interfixation, 31, 61, 70, 71, 72
Labio-Dental Fricative, 8
Lexemes, 6, 12, 17
Lexicon, 5
Locative, 95, 106, 107
Minimal Pairs, 6
Morphemes, 13, 14, 17, 18, 19, 20, 21, 31, 71, 86, 91, 97, 99, 143
Morphological Process, 11, 14, 17
Morphology, 13, 14, 16, 17, 19, 29, 30, 33, 37, 57, 68, 142
Motive, 95, 103, 104
Nasalization, 5, 8, 29
Negation, 21
Nominal Compound, 31
Nominal Derivation, 22
Nominalization, 30, 31

Nominal-Verbal, 6
Nomino-Verbals, 6, 62
Non-Expanded Vowels, 6, 43, 44, 52, 56, 58, 63, 64, 100, 101, 102, 103, 105, 106, 107, 108, 109, 112, 113, 114, 115, 116, 117, 118, 120, 123, 140
Non-Inflectional, 15, 29
Noun Agent, 30, 78
Noun Instrument, 79, 80
Noun Of Result, 74, 81
Number, 20
Operand, 14
Part Of Speech, 12, 30, 32, 36, 99
Participial, 6, 45, 46, 51, 52, 53, 54, 55, 56, 57, 84, 139, 140, 141, 142
Participle, 6, 25, 52, 61, 62, 66, 67, 135, 136, 137, 138, 139, 140, 141, 142
Perfective Affirmative, 51, 52, 53, 54, 55, 56, 57, 134, 139, 140
Phoneme, 5, 6, 7, 8
Phonological Features, 2, 5
Prefixation, 61, 62, 68, 69, 77
Qualificative, 81
Reduplication, 29, 30, 31, 61, 68, 69, 70, 142
Reflexives, 95, 114
Retaliative, 95, 115
Retracted Vowel, 7
Revisory, 95, 114
Root, 7, 11, 13, 14, 15, 17, 18, 19, 23, 24, 26, 29, 30, 31, 32, 34, 36, 37, 38, 39, 41, 42, 43, 44, 46, 47, 48, 49, 50, 51, 53, 54, 55, 56, 61, 62, 63, 64, 66, 68, 69, 70, 71, 72, 73, 74, 77, 78, 79, 84, 86, 95, 96, 97, 98, 101, 102, 105, 107, 109, 114, 115, 116, 119, 120, 121, 123, 124, 126, 128, 129, 135, 141, 143
Simple Gerunds, 77
Speech Community, 20
Stative Verb, 27
Stem, 12, 15
Subcategorization, 20
Suffixation, 20, 24, 31, 33, 34, 44, 61, 69, 70, 98
Superfix/Suprafix, 24
Superfixation, 20
Suprafixation, 20
Synthetic Compound, 31
Temporality, 95, 101
Tense, 17, 27, 32, 33, 37, 38, 62, 133
Terminative, 95, 100
Tone, 9, 24, 31, 35, 42, 43, 44, 45, 46, 48, 50, 51, 52, 53, 54, 55, 56, 57, 58, 61, 62, 63, 64, 67, 72, 74, 78, 79, 80, 81, 85, 86, 87, 88, 89, 90, 91, 92, 93, 96, 97, 98, 99, 100, 101, 102, 105, 106, 109, 112, 114, 115, 117, 119, 123, 135, 138, 140, 141, 142
Verbal Compounding, 11
Verbal Derivative, 22
Vowel Harmony, 5, 7, 29, 30, 39, 79, 96, 100, 101, 103, 108, 109, 114, 115, 117, 118, 120, 123
Wide & Narrow Sets, 7
Word Classes, 12
Word-Formation Process, 11